At Issue

What Is the Impact of Digitizing Books?

Other Books in the At Issue Series:

At Issue

What Is the Impact of Digitizing Books?

Louise I. Gerdes, Book Editor

GREENHAVEN PRESS
A part of Gale, Cengage Learning

GALE
CENGAGE Learning

Detroit • New York • San Francisco • New Haven, Conn • Waterville, Maine • London

Elizabeth Des Chenes, *Director, Publishing Solutions*

For more information, contact:
Greenhaven Press
27500 Drake Rd.
Farmington Hills, MI 48331-3535
Or you can visit our Internet site at gale.cengage.com

Articles in Greenhaven Press anthologies are often edited for length to meet page requirements. In addition, original titles of these works are changed to clearly present the main thesis and to explicitly indicate the author's opinion. Every effort is made to ensure that Greenhaven Press accurately reflects the original intent of the authors. Every effort has been made to trace the owners of copyrighted material.

Cover image photograph reproduced by permission of Brand X Pictures.

LIBRARY OF CONGRESS CATALOGING-IN-PUBLICATION DATA

What is the impact of digitizing books? / Louise I. Gerdes, book editor.
   pages cm. -- (At issue)
   Includes bibliographical references and index.
   ISBN 978-0-7377-6165-8 (hardcover) -- ISBN 978-0-7377-6166-5 (pbk.)
   1. Books--Digitization--Social aspects. 2. Books and reading--Technological innovations--Social aspects. 3. Electronic books. 4. Electronic publishing. 5. Learning and scholarship--Technological innovations--Social aspects. I. Gerdes, Louise I., 1953-
   Z1003.W545 2013
   070.5'73--dc23

                                                                    2012049717

Printed in the United States of America
1 2 3 4 5 6 7 17 16 15 14 13

Contents

Introduction

Some are calling the rapid and widespread growth of digital technology a digital revolution. One of several controversies in the debate over the influence of digital technology is the impact of digitizing books. Those who support book digitization claim that the process will make more books available to more people at a lower cost. According to Jason Epstein, cofounder of On Demand Books, the traditional publishing model is costly and inefficient. Digitizing books eliminates the infrastructure of traditional publishing—printing large quantities of books, then warehousing and shipping them to book sellers. The process of creating and distributing digital books, on the other hand, is more efficient, he maintains. "You can store in theory every book ever written in whatever language at practically no cost," Epstein asserts, "and deliver that file practically anywhere on Earth at no cost. This has a revolutionary effect on the way books are made and distributed."[1] Others fear that digitization changes what people think of as a book. Mary Harrington, an associate at the Institute for the Future of the Book in London, claims that what makes a physical book valuable is that it is a fixed object. Thus, she reasons, the author must choose his or her words carefully, and the message can be universal. These qualities are inverted with a digital book. The Internet, she claims, is "boundless, never authoritative—there's always someone who has something to add." In her view, "because the Internet is boundless, intangible and not edited, you can never publish the definitive anything online."[2]

Supporters of digital technology claim that such views are archaic and equate such thinking with fears throughout history of technological change of any kind. Indeed, supporters

1. Quoted in Sarah Glazer, "Future of Books," *CQ Researcher*, May 29, 2009.
2. *Ibid.*

often remind those who fear the digital book that the Greek philosopher Socrates told his student Plato that mental abilities would be diminished by writing down the stories that were once memorized and recited. Digital advocates sometimes derisively note that people would not know of Socrates's concerns if Plato had not written of them in his famous *Dialogues*. These commentators must concede, however, that Socrates was a great thinker. To be compared to Socrates is thus no great insult. In many ways, such comparisons are themselves becoming cliché and like many clichés oversimplify what is in truth a complex issue.

Examples of historical oversimplifications of the impact of technological development abound. During the Industrial Revolution, for example, technological advances dramatically improved agricultural, mining, and manufacturing practices. These advancements led to unprecedented social and economic change. Indeed, historians claim that the Industrial Revolution led to unparalleled increases in the standard of living for ordinary people. Nevertheless, the Industrial Revolution exacerbated many social problems: the factory led to the rise of the modern city, where the emerging middle class may have indeed lived in never-before-seen luxury but factory workers lived in squalor. These factories also threatened the livelihoods of artisans who struggled to compete with low-cost factory goods created by less-skilled, low-wage labor. In fact, those who support technological advancement often call opponents "Luddites," an often misused term given to those artisans who attacked factories and destroyed machines during the Industrial Revolution. These artisans were not, as some claim, like ignorant villagers storming Dr. Frankenstein's castle; indeed, they engaged in what some historians call "collective bargaining by riot." The British government was forced to use the British military to end what were very organized attacks. Luddites did not have an irrational fear of the new technology; they were, in fact, organized labor responding to economic policies that threatened their livelihood.

What is more, while the era's prosperity and developments in modern science and sanitation did ultimately lead to increases in life expectancy, the resulting increase in population and unchecked manufacturing practices had a significant and negative impact on the environment. Activist efforts to control this impact more than one hundred and fifty years later have improved manufacturing and agricultural practices, but some claim the environmental damage is irreversible. Thus, while the technological advances brought by the Industrial Revolution have in many ways improved human life, they also created significant problems. Some people did in fact lose their livelihood, and positive social changes such as a living wage for adults, child labor laws, and control of industrial waste took years and the hard work of activists. In the same way, controversies surrounding the impact of digitizing books are not simply a debate between those who abhor technological change and those who believe that technological change should go unchecked. The impact of the digital revolution on publishing is complex, as the digital revolution has evolved alongside other significant social and economic changes. A review of the historical development of the book and the publishing industry is indeed reflective of the complexity of the digital book debate.

Despite Socrates's concerns, the development of the Greek alphabet over twenty-five hundred years ago did lead to the preservation of Greek thought and stories such as Homer's *The Odyssey* that would otherwise have been lost. For several centuries, great Greek texts and Christian theological books were hand-copied and preserved on parchment pages. In the fifteenth century, metalsmith Johannes Gutenberg invented the process of printing with changeable type. He constructed a wooden-screw printing press that transferred the cast type onto paper. Although Gutenberg's only large-scale printing was of the Gutenberg Bible, his invention ultimately made the mass production of books possible, and as the process spread across Europe, books become more accessible and less costly. However, claims about the role this invention played in literacy and enlightened thought are sometimes exaggerated, as these social changes were long in coming and reflect a convergence of other significant developments.

While the invention of the printing press was indeed important, social, political, and economic changes altered who and what people read. The first books to appear in print shops were Bibles, religious tracts, and texts brought back from Byzantium during the Crusades. Few new ideas were printed. Moreover, the availability of books was not widespread and the Catholic Church generally controlled book content. However, from the late sixteenth through the early eighteenth centuries, the Protestant Reformation challenged the power of the Catholic Church, the Enlightenment increased the importance of science, and global exploration changed the way people looked at the world and in turn how it was represented. As a result, books became not passive objects but tools of personal, scientific, and global exploration.

Publishing began to develop as an industry during the eighteenth and nineteenth centuries. Indeed, during this time, the United States had established book printers in Boston, Cambridge, and Philadelphia. The construction of the Erie Canal, however, made it difficult for these cities to compete with New York publishers, who could ship books for less by using the canal. Thus, the canal helped establish New York as the major seat of publishing in America. Although there have been minor technological developments, publishing in the United States has changed little in over two hundred years. Book copy is delivered to a printer, who produces the printed book and ships the inventory to a warehouse, from which it is distributed to bookstores. The technological developments that made the process more efficient worried some, like those traditionalists today who dislike digital books. The creation of the steam press and stereotype plates made it possible to produce greater quantities of a book for less cost. Critics claimed that machine-made books were of inferior quality to those bound by hand.

It was during the development of the publishing industry that concerns arose about the pirating of books. Book piracy, the selling of books without payment to the publisher and author, is nothing new. In these early years, however, established American publishers, not unscrupulous digital entrepreneurs, pirated books. With a vast ocean between America and Great Britain, publishers could easily pirate the works of British authors such as Charles Dickens, William Thackeray, and the Brontë sisters. In fact, as Dickens's books gained popularity in America, he crossed the Atlantic to protest the theft of his property without success. By the end of the century, however, American authors sought protection for their work in foreign editions, and Congress passed the International Copyright Act to protect the work of all authors. However, these laws also granted publishers the right to sell specific books by specific authors, which also made publishers the content gatekeepers.

Publishing in the United States reached its peak at the beginning of the twentieth century. Indeed, the 1920s are referred to as the golden age of American publishing, and many publishing houses that emerged during this period were still strong in the 1950s. These publishing houses introduced American readers to the great writers of the day. In fact, between 1910 and 1940, illiteracy in America declined from 7.7 percent to 2.9 percent of the population. The number of libraries grew and people flocked to urban bookstores. The Book of the Month Club, founded in 1926, also increased readership, as did the launch of low-cost paperback editions. However the introduction of a new technological development, television, would reduce the primacy of reading in the middle of the century. Other social changes would once again impact the story of the book.

By the mid-1970s, many people began to migrate to the suburbs. With a reduced customer base, urban bookstores with large inventories of "backlist" titles—books other than new releases or current bestsellers—were forced to reduce their inventories. Suburban bookstores needed to have a quick turnover to make money and thus would sell mostly bestsellers or celebrity books. Publishing houses, however, depended on the ability of independent bookstores to sell backlists. When the backlists of these stores declined, publishing houses were forced to pay high advances and guarantees to bestselling authors and cut back on money spent to develop new talent. Between 1986 and 1996, sixty-three of the one hundred best-selling titles were written by only six writers—Tom Clancy, John Grisham, Stephen King, Dean Koontz, Michael Crichton, and Danielle Steel. To remain economically viable, publishing houses were incorporated into entertainment conglomerates. By the beginning of the twenty-first century, publishing in the United States was dominated by five global entertainment empires.

By the end of the first decade of the twenty-first century, the publishing industry was in collapse. In November 2008, Houghton Mifflin Harcourt, as well as other publishing houses, announced a buying freeze on new manuscripts. In December of that year, Penguin and Harper-Collins announced pay freezes, and Random House dissolved Doubleday and Bantam Dell. According to Samuel Freedman, author and professor at Columbia School of Journalism, "To be a journalist or author these days in America is to be a lumberjack in Wisconsin in the 1930s or a steelworker in Pennsylvania in the 1980s or an auto worker in Michigan, well, right now. It is to be watching your industry, and indeed your way of life, collapsing around you."[3] Some blame the publishing industry's

3. Samuel Freedman, "The Jerusalem Post," March 5, 2009.

collapse on its refusal to understand modern markets and thus change its practices. Many "midlist" authors, who have not achieved bestseller status, have little sympathy for publishing industry complaints against digital giants such as Amazon and Google. These authors claim that the publishing industry created its own monopoly over content and made making a living as a writer nearly impossible. According to independent author Catherine Czerkawska, "No matter what big publishers may say in their own justification . . . , the experience of most writers—even those with agents—is that editors are now almost wholly ruled and overruled by their marketing departments and those marketing departments are looking for instant gratification in the shape of a quick and easy bestseller."[4]

In this climate, amidst global social and economic change, the digital book emerged, and with it many of the concerns raised centuries before. Thus, in the way of the Industrial Revolution and the invention of the printing press, some believe that the digitizing of books will create a world-altering digital information revolution, in which all will have access to the world's printed knowledge. Others claim that this dream can only become a reality if governments and institutions support full and free access to published content. Granting a monopoly for the dispensing of the world's books to large corporations gives other analysts pause. Like the artisans of the industrial age, professional authors are concerned that their work has little value if publishers do not support them. Some authors fear that like the early American publishing houses, digital pirates will profit from their books. Others reason that the creative destruction that results from technological revolutions will lead to new forms of work. In fact, many authors, frustrated by a lack of support from a publishing industry beholden to stockholders, now publish their own books

---

4. Catherine Czerkawska, "Weeping Crocodiles: The Great eBook Debate," Wordarts .com, January 31, 2012. http://wordarts.blogspot.com/2012/01/weeping-crocodiles-great-ebook-debate.html.

online without the expense and gatekeeping of agents, editors, and traditional book publishers.

In the end, few claim that the digital book itself will change the world. The digital book is, like the printing press, an object. Social, political, and economic developments will, as they have in the past, exert their influence. In truth, readers, writers, scholars, content providers and curators, and technological innovators and entrepreneurs will determine the impact of digitizing books. Numerous perspectives on this issue are offered by the contributors of *At Issue: What Is the Impact of Digitizing Books?*

1

The Digital Age Has Not Significantly Changed the Way People Read

Robert Darnton

Robert Darnton is a cultural historian, professor, and university librarian at Harvard University. He is a leading expert on eighteenth-century France, a pioneer in the history of the book, and founder in 1999 of the Gutenberg Project, an e-book program designed to promote high-quality scholarly publishing on the Internet.

Misconceptions about the impact of digital technology and digitized books are widespread. In truth, new technologies strengthen rather than undermine the written word. The book is not dead; in fact, each year more books are published. Just as radio did not replace the newspaper and the Internet did not put an end to television, digital communication has not eliminated the reading of books. In fact, electronic books may actually stimulate reading. The claim that deep reading has declined is also unwarranted; deep reading among general readers has never been common. Moreover, people should be able to read in ways that are meaningful for them. In fact, digital books that include multimedia content and other features offer readers new ways to find meaning in books.

Robert Darnton, "5 Myths About the 'Information Age,'" *Chronicle of Higher Education*, April 17, 2011. Copyright © 2011 by Robert Darnton. All rights reserved. Reproduced by permission.

Confusion about the nature of the so-called information age has led to a state of collective false consciousness. It's no one's fault but everyone's problem, because in trying to get our bearings in cyberspace, we often get things wrong, and the misconceptions spread so rapidly that they go unchallenged. Taken together, they constitute a font of proverbial nonwisdom. Five stand out:

Five Myths of the Information Age

1. *"The book is dead."* Wrong: More books are produced in print each year than in the previous year. One million new titles will appear worldwide in 2011. In one day in Britain—"Super Thursday," last October 1 [2010]—800 new works were published. The latest figures for the United States cover only 2009, and they do not distinguish between new books and new editions of old books. But the total number, 288,355, suggests a healthy market, and the growth in 2010 and 2011 is likely to be much greater. Moreover, these figures, furnished by Bowker, do not include the explosion in the output of "nontraditional" books—a further 764,448 titles produced by self-publishing authors and "micro-niche" print-on-demand enterprises. And the book business is booming in developing countries like China and Brazil. However it is measured, the population of books is increasing, not decreasing, and certainly not dying.

2. *"We have entered the information age."* This announcement is usually intoned solemnly, as if information did not exist in other ages. But every age is an age of information, each in its own way and according to the media available at the time. No one would deny that the modes of communication are changing rapidly, perhaps

as rapidly as in Gutenberg's day, but it is misleading to construe that change as unprecedented.[1]

3. *"All information is now available online."* The absurdity of this claim is obvious to anyone who has ever done research in archives. Only a tiny fraction of archival material has ever been read, much less digitized. Most judicial decisions and legislation, both state and federal, have never appeared on the Web. The vast output of regulations and reports by public bodies remains largely inaccessible to the citizens it affects. Google estimates that 129,864,880 different books exist in the world, and it claims to have digitized 15 million of them—or about 12 percent. How will it close the gap while production continues to expand at a rate of a million new works a year? And how will information in nonprint formats make it online en masse? Half of all films made before 1940 have vanished. What percentage of current audiovisual material will survive, even in just a fleeting appearance on the Web? Despite the efforts to preserve the millions of messages exchanged by means of blogs, e-mail, and handheld devices, most of the daily flow of information disappears. Digital texts degrade far more easily than words printed on paper. Brewster Kahle, creator of the Internet Archive, calculated in 1997 that the average life of a URL was 44 days. Not only does most information not appear online, but most of the information that once did appear has probably been lost.

4. *"Libraries are obsolete."* Everywhere in the country librarians report that they have never had so many patrons. At Harvard, our reading rooms are full. The 85 branch libraries of the New York Public Library system are

---

1. Johannes Gutenberg was a German goldsmith and printer who invented movable type, which is widely regarded as the most important event following the Middle Ages, as printing ultimately made it possible for all to read and learn.

crammed with people. The libraries supply books, videos, and other material as always, but they also are fulfilling new functions: access to information for small businesses, help with homework and afterschool activities for children, and employment information for job seekers (the disappearance of want ads in printed newspapers makes the library's online services crucial for the unemployed). Librarians are responding to the needs of their patrons in many new ways, notably by guiding them through the wilderness of cyberspace to relevant and reliable digital material. Libraries never were warehouses of books. While continuing to provide books in the future, they will function as nerve centers for communicating digitized information at the neighborhood level as well as on college campuses.

5. *"The future is digital."* True enough, but misleading. In 10, 20, or 50 years, the information environment will be overwhelmingly digital, but the prevalence of electronic communication does not mean that printed material will cease to be important. Research in the relatively new discipline of book history has demonstrated that new modes of communication do not displace old ones, at least not in the short run. Manuscript publishing actually expanded after Gutenberg and continued to thrive for the next three centuries. Radio did not destroy the newspaper; television did not kill radio; and the Internet did not make TV extinct. In each case, the information environment became richer and more complex. That is what we are experiencing in this crucial phase of transition to a dominantly digital ecology.

Understanding Shifts in the Information Environment

I mention these misconceptions because I think they stand in the way of understanding shifts in the information environment. They make the changes appear too dramatic. They present things ahistorically and in sharp contrasts—before and after, either/or, black and white. A more nuanced view would reject the common notion that old books and e-books occupy opposite and antagonistic extremes on a technological spectrum. Old books and e-books should be thought of as allies, not enemies. To illustrate this argument, I would like to make some brief observations about the book trade, reading, and writing.

> *Ordinary readers ... appropriate books (including chapbooks and Harlequin romances) in their own ways, investing them with meaning that makes sense by their own lights.*

Last year [2010] the sale of e-books (digitized texts designed for hand-held readers) doubled, accounting for 10 percent of sales in the trade-book market. This year they are expected to reach 15 or even 20 percent. But there are indications that the sale of printed books has increased at the same time. The enthusiasm for e-books may have stimulated reading in general, and the market as a whole seems to be expanding. New book machines, which operate like ATM's, have reinforced this tendency. A customer enters a bookstore and orders a digitized text from a computer. The text is downloaded in the book machine, printed, and delivered as a paperback within four minutes. This version of print-on-demand shows how the old-fashioned printed codex can gain new life with the adaption of electronic technology.

The Impact on Reading

Many of us worry about a decline in deep, reflective, cover-to-cover reading. We deplore the shift to blogs, snippets, and tweets. In the case of research, we might concede that word searches have advantages, but we refuse to believe that they can lead to the kind of understanding that comes with the continuous study of an entire book. Is it true, however, that deep reading has declined, or even that it always prevailed? Studies by Kevin Sharpe, Lisa Jardine, and Anthony Grafton have proven that humanists in the 16th and 17th centuries often read discontinuously, searching for passages that could be used in the cut and thrust of rhetorical battles at court, or for nuggets of wisdom that could be copied into commonplace books and consulted out of context.

In studies of culture among the common people, Richard Hoggart and Michel de Certeau have emphasized the positive aspect of reading intermittently and in small doses. Ordinary readers, as they understand them, appropriate books (including chapbooks and Harlequin romances) in their own ways, investing them with meaning that makes sense by their own lights. Far from being passive, such readers, according to de Certeau, act as "poachers," snatching significance from whatever comes to hand.

A New Way of Writing

Writing looks as bad as reading to those who see nothing but decline in the advent of the Internet. As one lament puts it: Books used to be written for the general reader; now they are written by the general reader. The Internet certainly has stimulated self-publishing, but why should that be deplored? Many writers with important things to say had not been able to break into print, and anyone who finds little value in their work can ignore it.

> *The new technology is reinforcing old modes of communication rather than undermining them.*

The online version of the vanity press may contribute to the information overload, but professional publishers will provide relief from that problem by continuing to do what they always have done—selecting, editing, designing, and marketing the best works. They will have to adapt their skills to the Internet, but they are already doing so, and they can take advantage of the new possibilities offered by the new technology.

To use an example from my own experience, I recently wrote a printed book with an electronic supplement, *Poetry and the Police: Communication Networks in Eighteenth-Century Paris* (Harvard University Press). It describes how street songs mobilized public opinion in a largely illiterate society. Every day, Parisians improvised new words to old tunes, and the songs flew through the air with such force that they precipitated a political crisis in 1749. But how did their melodies inflect their meaning? After locating the musical annotations of a dozen songs, I asked a cabaret artist, Hélène Delavault, to record them for the electronic supplement. The reader can therefore study the text of the songs in the book while listening to them online. The e-ingredient of an old-fashioned codex makes it possible to explore a new dimension of the past by capturing its sounds.

One could cite other examples of how the new technology is reinforcing old modes of communication rather than undermining them. I don't mean to minimize the difficulties faced by authors, publishers, and readers, but I believe that some historically informed reflection could dispel the misconceptions that prevent us from making the most of "the information age"—if we must call it that.

2

Digitizing Books Will Change Publishing for the Better

Jason Epstein

Jason Epstein is an American editor and publisher who launched several paperback divisions while at Random House to make books more accessible. In 2007 he cofounded On Demand Books, which manufactures the Espresso Book Machine, a copier-sized device that can print and bind entire books in a few minutes.

Making books available digitally eliminates the costs of storing and delivering books—savings that publishers can pass on to the consumer. Efforts by publishers to impede this process are fruitless. Indeed, the US Justice Department is suing Apple and several major book publishers for price-fixing policies that prevent Amazon from determining the price of the e-books that it sells, a price far lower than publishers want to charge. Although some claim that the lawsuit effectively grants Amazon a monopoly on e-book sales, in the end the result impels publishers to abandon obsolete publishing practices and requires them to produce books more efficiently.

So far discussion of the Justice Department's suit against Apple and several major book publishers for conspiring to fix retail prices of e-books has omitted the major issue: the impact of digitization on the book industry generally. The immediate symptoms are Amazon's own pricing strategy—which,

Jason Epstein, "How Books Will Survive Amazon," *New York Review of Books*, April 26, 2012. *The New York Review of Books* blog, NYRblog (www.nybooks.com/blogs/nyrblog/). Copyright © 2012 by Jason Epstein.

unlike Apple's and the publishers', is to sell e-books below cost to achieve market share and perhaps a monopoly—and the federal suit challenging Apple's and the publishers' counterattack.

Hoping to Dominate the Digital Market

The revolutionary process by which all books, old and new, in all languages, will soon be available digitally, at practically no cost for storage and delivery, to a radically decentralized worldwide market at the click of a mouse is irreversible. The technologically obsolete system, in which physical inventory is stored in publishers' warehouses and trucked to fixed retail locations, will sooner or later be replaced by the more efficient digital alternative. The government's case against book publishers arises from this continuing transformation—Amazon's pricing model for e-books reflects the digital imperative while Apple's and the publishers' response attempts to delay it.

The problem began when Amazon set out to charge $9.99 per e-book download, considerably less than it was paying publishers for their e-book inventory. Since Amazon's competitors could not afford such a costly strategy, Amazon hoped to dominate (or even monopolize) the e-book market and dictate future e-book pricing. Should Amazon's $9.99 price become the industry standard—a reasonable assumption since e-books like iTunes are merely disembodied electronic information—publishers might then be obliged to sell e-book content to Amazon for perhaps as little as $6.00, too little to contribute their share of pre-digital legacy costs for warehousing, inventory and traditional marketing. Publishers, unable to support these residual costs by physical book sales alone, might eventually submit to the digital imperative and market their books directly to the web to be read on digital screens or printed on demand one copy at a time at diverse locations. Though Amazon's strategy, if successful, might force publishers to shrink or even abandon their old infrastructure, demand for physical books, printed and bound, will not disappear. Publishers might thus find it necessary to subcontract their physical inventory to specialized distributors.

Independent editorial start-ups posting their books on appropriate web sites have already begun to emerge and more will follow. The cost of entry will be slight. The essential capital will be editorial talent and energy, as it had been in the glory days before conglomeration when editors were themselves de facto publishers, publicists, and marketers. Many start-ups will fail. Some will not. Specificity, reflecting the structure of the web, will matter: a guide to the cultivation of daffodils will more likely succeed than a more diffuse gardening title.

> *[The] conflict between Amazon and publishers . . . is a vivid expression of how the logic of a radical new and more efficient technology impels institutional change.*

Amazon may also attempt to reduce or eliminate its own inventory expenses by printing orders for backlist titles on demand on its own presses. Traditional publishers have resisted this proposal and Amazon has responded by threatening not to stock slower-selling backlist titles.

Conspiring to Prevent a Monopoly

To counter Amazon's pricing policy, publishers have adopted the so-called agency pricing model, in which inventory is not sold to retailers, including Amazon, but consigned to them as agents who are compensated by a fee. Since Amazon in this scheme does not purchase content but acts only as the publishers' representative, it has no right to determine the retail price. This defense seems to have been suggested to the publishers by Steve Jobs, whose own products are sold either by Apple's own stores or by the agency method, and who did not want to match Amazon's costly strategy for his iPad e-book sales.

The Justice Department has sued Apple and the publishers not because the agency model is illegal—it is not—but because Apple and the publishers may illegally have conspired to adopt the agency model to restrain Amazon from creating a monopoly by determining its own pricing. The outcome of the Justice Department's suit is unclear: some publishers have settled with the Department of Justice, others have not.[1] But what seems inevitable is that this tangled web in which the government helped give Amazon a possible monopoly, will be chuckled over by law students and their professors for many years.

A Need for Institutional Change

The underlying issue is more significant than the lawsuit and its outcome. What matters is Amazon's attempt to force publishers to conform to the digital imperative by resisting prices that include traditional publishing costs. This is more than a conflict between Amazon and publishers. It is a vivid expression of how the logic of a radical new and more efficient technology impels institutional change.

Few technological victories are ever complete, and in the case of books this will be especially true. Bookstores will not disappear but will exploit digital technologies to increase their virtual and physical inventories, and perhaps become publishers themselves. So will libraries, whose vast and arcane holdings will soon be available to everyone everywhere. E-books have been aggressively marketed for five or six years in the United States. Yet despite rapidly acquiring market share they

1. As of this writing, three defendants in the federal investigation—Hachette Book Group, HarperCollins Publishers and Simon & Schuster—have agreed to settlement talks with US officials over the price-fixing charges. However, Apple and publishers Macmillan and Penguin have vowed to fight the charges in the district court. The trial is set for June 2013.

show no sign of displacing actual books, with which they will comfortably coexist in the digital future.

Today's publishers, still entangled in the dying Gutenberg[2] age, will, one hopes, spin off their talented editors as semi-autonomous units and gradually disencumber themselves of their obsolete infrastructure. Barring a nuclear disaster, life will go on as it always has: past, present, and future all at once.

2. Johannes Gutenberg was a German goldsmith and printer who invented movable type, which is widely regarded as the most important event following the Middle Ages, as printing ultimately made it possible for all to read and learn.

3

Digitizing Books Devalues the Work of Professional Writers

Ewan Morrison

Ewan Morrison, who after graduating from the Glasgow School of Art in Scotland was a television and short film director, is author of the novels Swung, Menage, *and* Distance *and a collection of short stories,* The Last Book You Read.

The publication of e-books will put an end to writing as a profession. Writers need economic support to produce quality content. However, e-book sellers are interested not in quality but in quantity. While traditional book publishers profit from the sale of quality books or books by popular authors, digital content providers profit from making more content available to more people. Moreover, online booksellers can sell books for much less than traditional publishers as they profit not from book sales but from selling consumer information to advertising companies. Unfortunately, since content has little value to digital booksellers, publishers are unwilling to nurture developing writers who are not already profitable. If the culture no longer values writing as a profession, then digital content service providers and advertisers, not professional writers, will determine content.

Will books, as we know them, come to an end?

Yes, absolutely, within 25 years the digital revolution will bring about the end of paper books. But more importantly, ebooks and e-publishing will mean the end of "the writer" as a profession. Ebooks, in the future, will be written by first-timers, by teams, by speciality subject enthusiasts and by those who were already established in the era of the paper book. The digital revolution will not emancipate writers or open up a new era of creativity, it will mean that writers offer up their work for next to nothing or for free. Writing, as a profession, will cease to exist.

Generation Y and the End of Paper Books

First of all I'd like to clear up the question: "The end of Books?" This is misleading as it seems purely technical—a question of the paper mill versus the hard drive. Of course the paper book will survive, you may say; it will reinvent itself as it did before. Haven't future projections been wrong in the past? Didn't they say Penguin paperbacks would destroy the print industry in 1939? That the printing press would overthrow Catholicism after 1440? That home videos would destroy cinema?

On the paper front, depending on whom you listen to, statistics vary wildy. Barnes and Noble claims it now sells three times as many digital books as all formats of physical books combined. Amazon claims it has crossed the tipping point and sells 242 ebooks for every 100 hardbacks, while Richard Sarnoff, CEO of Bertelsmann [a global media company], admits that the future of the paper book is tied to the consumption habits of a generation: the baby boomers. Generation Y-ers (the children of the boomers) already consume 78% of their news digitally, for free, and books will follow suit. Interpreting Sarnoff's calculations, the paper book has a generation left.

But let's leave the survival of the paper book alone, and ask the more important question: Will writers be able to make a living and continue writing in the digital era? And let's also leave alone the question: why should authors live by their work? Let's abandon the romantic myth that writers must survive in the garret, and look at the facts. Most notable writers in the history of books were paid a living wage: they include Dostoevksy, Dickens and Shakespeare. In the last 50 years the system of publishers' advances has supported writers such as Ian McEwan, Angela Carter, JM Coetzee, Joan Didion, Milan Kundera, Don DeLillo, Salman Rushdie, Norman Mailer, Philip Roth, Anita Shreve, Graham Greene, Muriel Spark and John Fowles. Authors do not live on royalties alone. To ask whether International Man Booker prizewinner Philip Roth could have written 24 novels and the award-winning American trilogy without advances is like asking if Michelangelo could have painted the Sistine Chapel without the patronage of Pope Julius II. The economic framework that supports artists is as important as the art itself; if you remove one from the other then things fall apart.

[Many writers have] come to believe that publishers and their distribution systems are out of date; that too many middle-men (distributors, booksellers) have been living off their work.

And this is what is happening now.

The Retreat of Advances

With the era of digital publishing and digital distribution, the age of author advances is coming to an end. Without advances from publishers, authors depend upon future sales; they sink themselves into debt on the chance of a future hit. But as mainstream publishers struggle to compete with digital competitors, they are moving increasingly towards maximising short-term profits, betting on the already-established, and away from nurturing talent. *The Bookseller* claimed in 2009 that "Publishers are cutting author advances by as much as 80% in the UK". A popular catchphrase among agents, when discussing advances, meanwhile, is "10K is the new 50K". And as one literary editor recently put it: "The days of publishing an author, as opposed to publishing a book, seem to be over."

Publishers are focusing on the short term and are dropping midlist writers. Midlisters—neither bestsellers nor first-timers—were formerly the Research and Development department of publishers in the 20th century. It was within the midlist that future award-winners and bestsellers were hot-housed (Don DeLillo, for example, was supported as a midlist author over the six underperforming books that preceded his Pulitzer-nominated, multi-award winning novel, *Underworld*.

In reaction to the removal of their living wage, many writers have decided to abandon the mainstream entirely: they've come to believe that publishers and their distribution systems are out of date; that too many middle-men (distributors, booksellers) have been living off their work. When authors either self e-publish or do deals through agents that go straight to digital they embrace a philosophy of the digital market called *the long tail*.

Living in the Long Tail

The long tail is best described by business adviser, futurologist, guru and editor of *Wired* magazine, Chris Anderson, in his book *The Long Tail, or Why the Future of Business is Selling Less of More*. An alternative tagline for the book is How Endless Choice is Creating Unlimited Demand. In simple terms, the long tail derives its name from graphs of sales against number of products. Whereas throughout the 20th century publishers concentrated on selling only a few heavily promoted "hits" or "bestsellers" in bulk, digital shopping has meant that what was originally a tail-off in sales, has now become increasingly profitable. Rather than selling, say, 13m [million] copies of one Harry Potter book, a long tail provider can make the same profits by selling 13m different "obscure", "failed'" and "niche" books.

The long tail is Amazon and iTunes, Netflix, LoveFilm and eBay. It is, arguably, between 40% to 60% of the market, which was hidden and/or simply unavailable before the advent of online shopping.

Writing has already begun its slide towards becoming something produced and consumed for free.

As more consumers come online and choose to select content for themselves, the long tail gets longer. It also starts to demolish the old mainstream system of pre-selection, mass marketing and limited shelf space for "bestsellers". Amazon is a successful long-tail industry: it has forced publishers into selling their books at 60% discount and driven bookshops out of business. As the long tail grows, the mainstream mass market shrinks and becomes more conservative. The long tail has created this effect in all of the other industries that have gone digital.

Myths of the Long Tail

The recent enthusiasm for the long-tail market does, however, obscure a very basic economic fact: very few writers and independent publishers can survive in the long tail. Amazon can sell millions of books by obscure authors, while at the same time those authors, when they get their Amazon receipts, will see that they have sold only five books in a year. This is not an accident, but part of a trend endemic to the digital world. As Chris Anderson said in his book *Free: Why $0.00 Is the Future of Business*: "Every industry that becomes Digital will eventually become free."

The reason why a living wage for writers is essential is that every industry that has become digital has seen a dramatic, and in many cases terminal, decrease in earnings for those who create "content". Writing has already begun its slide towards becoming something produced and consumed for free. . . .

The Free Revolution

For all its digital-friendly rhetoric and the co-option of "radical" jargon, surely the people at Google, Yahoo and YouTube aren't working for free. These companies are making a profit big enough to place them on the Fortune 500. So if the future of digital media is "free", where does the money come from?

While providers such as Yahoo and Google provide free content, at the same time, on every screen, they sell advertising space. The culture (books, films and music) that you find for free on the sites, is not the product, it has no monetary value. The real product Yahoo and Google are selling is something less tangible—it is you.

Forecasts predict that within 10 to 15 years the largest "publishers" in the world will be Google, Amazon and Apple.

Your profile and that of millions of other consumers are being sold to advertisers. Your hits and clicks make them money.

These digital providers are not in any way concerned with or interested in content, or what used to be called "culture". To them culture is merely generic content; it is a free service that is provided in the selling of customers to advertisers. Ideally for service providers, the customers will even provide the culture themselves, for free. And this is what we do when we write blogs, or free ebooks or upload films of ourselves, at no cost.

Forecasts predict that within 10 to 15 years the largest "publishers" in the world will be Google, Amazon and Apple. In May 2010, Google announced plans to compete with Amazon, Barnes and Noble and Apple by launching its own online ebook store, which requires no e-reader and no fees. In August of the same year, Google announunced its intention to scan all known books (130m) by the end of the decade. All of which would be available for free or for a minuscule one-off payment to authors of around $60 per book. Google is still caught up in legal wrangles, but this change is coming.

Piracy and Competitive Discounting— The Race to the Bottom

Back again to books. In all of the cases above, digital industries have been pushed towards zero price by two factors: (1) mass piracy and (2) the consumer demand for massive discounts. Book piracy has only just begun but it is now very simple to break through the DRM [digital rights management] protection systems set up by publishers and to illegally download books in less than 60 seconds. The shift to piracy moves imperceptibly in the mind of the consumer, as Adrian Hon, founder of a leading games company outlined in the *Telegraph*.

Will digital books be any different from jpegs, quicktimes and mp3s? What makes them so, other than a desire by the currently dominant generation to preserve what they have known.

It starts in this way: consumers download electronic copies of books that they already own for convenience sake (an activity that the *New York Times* claims is ethical). This introduces people to ebook torrents. Then they start downloading classics: "Tolkien and CS Lewis are both dead, so why should I feel bad about pirating their books?" And since they have enough memory on their e-reader to store 3,500 books and the e-reader came with four preloaded free classics to start with, what difference will it make? Then, says Hon, "you'll have people downloading ebooks not available in their country yet. Then it'll be people downloading entire collections, just because it's quicker. Then they'll start wondering why they should buy any ebooks at all, when they cost so much."

In every digital industry the attempt to combat piracy has led to a massive reduction in cover price: the slippery slope towards free digital content.

Will digital books be any different from jpegs, quicktimes and mp3s? What makes them so, other than a desire by the currently dominant generation to preserve what they have known—a trend that will be outgrown when that generation passes?

The Long Term Against the Long Tail

Is there an alternative to this catastrophe? If so, it cannot lie where Chris Anderson recommends, in having what he terms "freemium viewing"—locked or extra content for subscribers (a system devised for newspapers and computer games). What would this mean for the book? An extra chapter? An author's commentary? The final sentence if you pay more?

For authors and publishers to abandon each other only accelerates the race towards free content.

An alternative could lie in authors writing apps and blogs, on both of which, the author would get paid per 10,000 or so hits, by advertisers. Or it could lie in crowd funding—with innovations such as publishing house 'Unbound'. You have enough readers, they pay a dollar or a pound, and en masse they see you through the duration required to write the book, that you then give them for free.

The trend of consumers demanding ever more for ever less is not restricted to culture. It's a phenomenon well documented by writers such as Zygmunt Bauman and Naomi Klein:

the "race to the bottom", in which competing corporations cut their prices in the bid to put all other competitors out of business.

Can Books Be Written in Sweatshops?

Well, books might not be manufactured in China and Korea but the long tail is the sweatshop of the future, and it will contain millions of would-be-writers who will labour under the delusion that they can be successful in the way writers were before, in the age of the mainstream and the paper book.

There is no simple solution. All that is clear is that for authors and publishers to abandon each other only accelerates the race towards free content.

Authors must respect and demand the work of good editors and support the publishing industry, precisely by resisting the temptation to "go it alone" in the long tail. In return, publishing houses must take the risk on the long term; supporting writers over years and books, it is only then that books of the standard we have seen in the last half-century can continue to come into being.

This is something that publishers are well aware of, but still seem powerless to do anything about. As Sarnoff CEO of Bertelsmann has said, ". . . as things switch to digital there is the danger that a lot of value can leak out of the industry, and that our authors, our artists won't have enough revenues there to pay for their best work and that we won't have enough revenue to pay for our own infrastructure."

I ask you to take the long view, to look a generation beyond where we are now, and to express concern for the future of the book.

If the connection between publishers and writers splits completely, if they fail to support and defend each other, then both will separately be subjected to the markets' demand for totally free content, and both shall have very short lives in the long tail. The writer will become an entrepreneur with a short shelf life, in a world without publishers or even shelves.

But ultimately, any strategy conceived now is just playing for time as the slide towards a totally free digital culture accelerates. How long have we got? A generation. After that, writers, like musicians, filmmakers, critics, porn stars, journalists and photographers, will have to find other ways of making a living in a short-term world that will not pay them for their labour.

The only solution ultimately is a political one. As we grow increasingly disillusioned with quick-fix consumerism, we may want to consider an option which exists in many non-digital industries: quite simply, demanding that writers get paid a living wage for their work. Do we respect the art and craft of writing enough to make such demands? If we do not, we will have returned to the garret, only this time, the writer will not be alone in his or her cold little room, and will be writing to and for a computer screen, trying to get hits on their site that will draw the attention of the new culture lords—the service providers and the advertisers.

I ask you to take the long view, to look a generation beyond where we are now, and to express concern for the future of the book. I ask you to vote that the end of "the book" as written by professional writers, is imminent; and not to be placated with short-term projections and enthusiasms intended to reduce fear in a confused market. I ask you to leave this place troubled, and to ask yourself and as many others as you can, what you can do if you truly value the work of the people formerly known as writers.

4

The Ability to Revise Digitized Books Yields Benefits and Risks

Nicholas Carr

Nicholas Carr writes about technology, culture, and economics for The Atlantic, The New York Times, Wall Street Journal, Wired, The Times of London, *and* The New Republic. *He is author of* The Shallows: What the Internet Is Doing to Our Brains.

While the content of traditional, printed books is fixed, digital books are more malleable. The ability to change text once an electronic book is published has both benefits and risks. Writers can revise at any time to correct errors, update facts, add new supporting evidence, or acknowledge recent events. The risk, however, is that people in positions of authority can edit what people read. Thus, school boards can remove content they believe to be objectionable and authoritarian governments can edit content to serve political ends. Of greater concern is that reading will be controlled by the market, thus devaluing the book as a finite and independent work of art. Nevertheless, editable digital books seem destined to replace printed books.

I recently got a glimpse into the future of books. A few months ago, I dug out a handful of old essays I'd written about innovation, combined them into a single document, and uploaded the file to Amazon's Kindle Direct Publishing service. Two days later, my little e-book was on sale at Amazon's site. The whole process couldn't have been simpler.

Then I got the urge to tweak a couple of sentences in one of the essays. I made the edits on my computer and sent the revised file back to Amazon. The company quickly swapped out the old version for the new one. I felt a little guilty about changing a book after it had been published, knowing that different readers would see different versions of what appeared to be the same edition. But I also knew that the readers would be oblivious to the alterations.

An e-book, I realized, is far different from an old-fashioned printed one. The words in the latter stay put. In the former, the words can keep changing, at the whim of the author or anyone else with access to the source file. The endless malleability of digital writing promises to overturn a whole lot of our assumptions about publishing.

Typographical Fixity

When Johannes Gutenberg invented movable type a half-millennium ago, he also gave us immovable text. Before Gutenberg, books were handwritten by scribes, and no two copies were exactly the same. Scribes weren't machines; they made mistakes. With the arrival of the letterpress, thousands of identical copies could enter the marketplace simultaneously. The publication of a book, once a nebulous process, became an event.

[Digitizing books] makes it easy for writers to correct errors and update facts.

A new set of literary workers coalesced in publishing houses, collaborating with writers to perfect texts before they went on press. The verb "to finalize" became common in literary circles, expressing the permanence of printed words. Different editions still had textual variations, introduced either intentionally as revisions or inadvertently through sloppy editing or typesetting, but books still came to be viewed, by writer and reader alike, as immutable objects. They were written for posterity.

Beyond giving writers a spur to eloquence, what the historian Elizabeth Eisenstein calls "typographical fixity" served as a cultural preservative. It helped to protect original documents from corruption, providing a more solid foundation for the writing of history. It established a reliable record of knowledge, aiding the spread of science. It accelerated the standardization of everything from language to law. The preservative qualities of printed books, Ms. Eisenstein argues, may be the most important legacy of Gutenberg's invention.

The Benefits of Endless Malleability

Once digitized, a page of words loses its fixity. It can change every time it's refreshed on a screen. A book page turns into something like a Web page, able to be revised endlessly after its initial uploading. There's no technological constraint on perpetual editing, and the cost of altering digital text is basically zero. As electronic books push paper ones aside, movable type seems fated to be replaced by movable text.

Authoritarian governments will be able to tweak books to suit their political interests.

That's an attractive development in many ways, it makes it easy for writers to correct errors and update facts. Guidebooks will no longer send travelers to restaurants that have closed or to once charming inns that have turned into fleabags. The instructions in manuals will always be accurate. Reference books need never go out of date.

Even literary authors will be tempted to keep their works fresh. Historians and biographers will be able to revise their narratives to account for recent events or newly discovered documents. Polemicists will be able to bolster their arguments with new evidence. Novelists will be able to scrub away the little anachronisms that can make even a recently published story feel dated.

The Risk of Abuse

But as is often the case with digitization, the boon carries a bane. The ability to alter the contents of a book will be easy to abuse. School boards may come to exert even greater influence over what students read. They'll be able to edit textbooks that don't fit with local biases. Authoritarian governments will be able to tweak books to suit their political interests. And the edits can ripple backward. Because e-readers connect to the Internet, the works they contain can be revised remotely, just as software programs are updated today. Movable text makes a lousy preservative.

Such abuses can be prevented through laws and software protocols. What may be more insidious is the pressure to fiddle with books for commercial reasons. Because e-readers gather enormously detailed information on the way people read, publishers may soon be awash in market research. They'll know how quickly readers progress through different chapters, when they skip pages, and when they abandon a book.

The promise of stronger sales and profits will make it hard to resist tinkering with a book in response to such signals, adding a few choice words here, trimming a chapter there, maybe giving a key character a quick makeover. What will be lost, or at least diminished, is the sense of a book as a finished and complete object, a self-contained work of art.

Not long before he died, John Updike spoke eloquently of a book's "edges," the boundaries that give shape and integrity to a literary work and that for centuries have found their outward expression in the indelibility of printed pages. It's those edges that give a book its solidity, allowing it to stand up to the vagaries of fashion and the erosions of time. And it's those edges that seem fated to blur as the words of books go from being stamped permanently on sheets of paper to being rendered temporarily on flickering screens.

5

Digitizing Historical Texts Eliminates the Thrill of Scholarship

Tristram Hunt

Tristram Hunt is a British Labour Party politician, activist, historian, and broadcaster, who lectures on modern British history at Queen Mary, University of London. Hunt writes regularly for the Observer.

Although publishing digital copies of historical documents will improve the speed of scholarship, some of the mystery and thrill of scholarship is lost when studying digital copies. The meaning of the words and the passion of the writer is best learned by holding the original manuscript. Indeed, the chance of finding something previously undiscovered is more likely with the original source than an electronic copy. Moreover, nothing compares to the excitement of leafing through an original historical document.

It was discovered in 1907, walled up in a cave on the Silk Road in Dunhuang, north-west China, where it had lain untouched for 900 years. *The Diamond Sutra*, dated "the 13th of the fourth moon of the ninth year of Xiatong" or 868AD, is a sacred text of the Buddhist faith and one of the hidden treasures of the British Library [BL]. Or not so hidden, as it can now be downloaded as a smartphone app.

Short Cuts for Interpreting the Past

The ubiquity of history has taken another huge step forward with the BL-Google tie-up putting some 250,000 books online. An astonishing range of texts from 1700 to 1870, covering the French Revolution, the Enlightenment, the early days of empire and the Industrial Revolution, will soon be accessible via Google Book Search. From a Mumbai coffee-shop or Australian air terminal, we will all be able to mull over such wonders as George-Louis Leclerc's 1775 treatise, *The Natural History of the Hippopotamus, or River Horse.*

The Google partnership signals an undoubted advance for scholarship. For the arrival of search engines has transformed our ability to sift and surf the past. What once would have required days trawling through an index, hunting down a footnote or finding a misfiled library book can now be done in an instant. Want to find a reference by [Karl] Marx to [William] Gladstone? Not a problem at www.marxists.org. Want to find the chattels left by Georgina, Duchess of Devonshire? The online Dictionary of National Biography has the answer.

It is only with [manuscript] in hand that the real meaning of the text becomes apparent: its rhythms and cadences, the relationship of image to word, the passion of the argument or cold logic of the case.

This techno-enthusiasm should not come as too much of a surprise. For all their fusty reputation, historians are very keen on short cuts for interpreting the past. In the 1970s, the "econometricians" embraced IBM mainframes as a way of crunching data on development. In the 1980s, it was all about placing the Domesday Book on CD-ROMS. Now, no museum experience is complete without an accompanying app, while GPS has transformed battlefield studies. Historians have also fallen for the blog, a perfect vehicle for the lifeblood of gossip, envy, malice and "constructive criticism" that keeps history happening.

Losing the Mystery of History

Yet when everything is down-loadable, the mystery of history can be lost. Why sit in an archive leafing through impenetrable prose when you can slurp frappucino while scrolling down Edmund Burke [an Irish statesman and philosopher] documents?

But it is only with MS [manuscript] in hand that the real meaning of the text becomes apparent: its rhythms and cadences, the relationship of image to word, the passion of the argument or cold logic of the case. Then there is the serendipity, the scholar's eternal hope that something will catch his eye. Perhaps another document will come up in the same batch, perhaps some marginalia or even the leaf of another text inserted as a bookmark. There is nothing more thrilling than untying the frayed string, opening the envelope and leafing through a first edition in the expectation of unexpected discoveries. None of that is possible on an iPad.

In a lecture, [English historian of government] Peter Hennessy recently described the historian's craft as akin to the cryogenic trade—warming up the frozen history of the archive until it began to talk. Such a delicate procedure is usually best performed by hand.

6

Digitizing Historical Texts Does Not Demean Scholarship

James Gleick

James Gleick is a science history writer, biographer, and author of The Information: A History, a Theory, a Flood, *which covers the genesis of the information age.*

The claim that true scholarship can only be achieved by reading original manuscripts is misguided sentimentalism. That people often associate an object's value with its scarcity obscures the fact that the ideas within, not the manuscript itself, make a document valuable. Making these texts more widely available to scholars will improve rather than impede scholarship. While scholars should continue to value the original, the real power of the document is in the words, which should be accessible to all.

I got a real thrill in December 1999 in the Reading Room of the Morgan Library in New York when the librarian, Sylvie Merian, brought me, after I had completed an application with a letter of reference and a photo ID, the first, oldest notebook of Isaac Newton. First I was required to study a microfilm version. There followed a certain amount of appropriate pomp. The notebook was lifted from a blue cloth drop-spine box and laid on a special padded stand. I was struck by how impossibly tiny it was—58 leaves bound in vellum, just 2 3/4 inches wide, half the size I would have guessed from the enlarged microfilm images. There was his name, "Isacus Newton," proudly inscribed by the 17-year-old with his quill, and the date, 1659.

"He filled the pages with meticulous script, the letters and numerals often less than one-sixteenth of an inch high," I wrote in my book "Isaac Newton" a few years later. "He began at both ends and worked toward the middle."

Apparently historians know the feeling well—the exhilaration that comes from handling the venerable original. It's a contact high. In this time of digitization, it is said to be endangered. The Morgan Notebook of Isaac Newton is online now (thanks to the Newton Project at the University of Sussex). You can surf it.

The raw material of history appears to be heading for the cloud. What once was hard is now easy. What was slow is now fast.

Is this a case of "be careful what you wish for"?

Some of the qualms about digital research reflect a feeling that anything obtained too easily loses its value. What we work for, we better appreciate.

The New Renaissance

Last month [June 2011] the British Library announced a project with Google to digitize 40 million pages of books, pamphlets and periodicals dating to the French Revolution. The European Digital Library, Europeana.eu, well surpassed its initial goal of 10 million "objects" last year, including a Bulgarian parchment manuscript from 1221 and the Rok runestone from Sweden, circa 800, which will save you trips to, respectively, the St. Cyril and St. Methodius National Library in Sofia and a church in Ostergotland.

Reporting to the European Union in Brussels, the Comité des Sages (sounds better than "Reflection Group") urged in January that essentially everything—all the out-of-copyright cultural heritage of all the member states—should be digitized and made freely available online. It put the cost at approximately $140 billion and called this vision "The New Renaissance."

Inevitably comes the backlash. Where some see enrichment, others see impoverishment. Tristram Hunt, an English historian and member of Parliament, complained in *The Observer* this month that "techno-enthusiasm" threatens to cheapen scholarship. "When everything is downloadable, the mystery of history can be lost," he wrote. "It is only with MS [manuscript] in hand that the real meaning of the text becomes apparent: its rhythms and cadences, the relationship of image to word, the passion of the argument or cold logic of the case."

The Fetishization of Historical Texts

I'm not buying this. I think it's sentimentalism, and even fetishization. It's related to the fancy that what one loves about books is the grain of paper and the scent of glue.

Some of the qualms about digital research reflect a feeling that anything obtained too easily loses its value. What we work for, we better appreciate. If an amateur can be beamed to the top of Mount Everest, will the view be as magnificent as for someone who has accomplished the climb? Maybe not, because magnificence is subjective. But it's the same view.

Another worry is the loss of serendipity—as Mr. Hunt says, "the scholar's eternal hope that something will catch his eye." When you open a book Newton once owned, which you can do (by appointment) in the library of Trinity College, Cambridge, you may see notes he scribbled in the margins. But marginalia are being digitized, too. And I find that online discovery leads to unexpected twists and turns of research at least as often as the same time spent in archives.

It's a mistake to deprecate digital images just because they are suddenly everywhere, reproduced so effortlessly.

Inspiring New Scholarship

"New Renaissance" may be a bit of hype, but a profound transformation lies ahead for the practice of history. Europeans seem to have taken the lead in creating digital showcases; maybe they just have more history to work with than Americans do. One brilliant new resource among many is the London Lives project: 240,000 manuscript and printed pages dating to 1690, focusing on the poor, including parish archives, records from workhouses and hospitals, and trial proceedings from the Old Bailey.

Storehouses like these, open to anyone, will surely inspire new scholarship. They enrich cyberspace, particularly because without them the online perspective is so foreshortened, so locked into the present day. Not that historians should retire to their computer terminals; the sights and smells of history, where we can still find them, are to be cherished. But the artifact is hardly a clear window onto the past; a window, yes, clouded and smudged like all the rest.

It's a mistake to deprecate digital images just because they are suddenly everywhere, reproduced so effortlessly. We're in the habit of associating value with scarcity, but the digital world unlinks them. You can be the sole owner of a Jackson Pollock or a Blue Mauritius but not of a piece of information—not for long, anyway. Nor is obscurity a virtue. A hidden parchment page enters the light when it molts into a digital simulacrum. It was never the parchment that mattered.

Oddly, for collectors of antiquities, the pricing of informational relics seems undiminished by cheap reproduction—

maybe just the opposite. In a Sotheby's auction three years ago, Magna Carta fetched a record $21 million. To be exact, the venerable item was a copy of Magna Carta, made 82 years after the first version was written and sealed at Runnymede. Why is this tattered parchment valuable? Magical thinking. It is a talisman. The precious item is a trick of the eye. The real Magna Carta, the great charter of human rights and liberty, is available free online, where it is safely preserved. It cannot be lost or destroyed.

An object like this—a talisman—is like the coffin at a funeral. It deserves to be honored, but the soul has moved on.

7

No Company Should Be Allowed a Monopoly on Book Digitization

Brewster Kahle

Brewster Kahle is a computer engineer, digital librarian, Internet entrepreneur, and advocate of universal access to knowledge. He is founder and director of the Internet Archive, a nonprofit library in San Francisco, and of the Open Content Alliance, an organization whose goal is to build a permanent archive of multilingual digitized text and multimedia material.

All people should have access to knowledge. Granting companies such as Google the rights to sell access to books that are not subject to copyright laws will limit public access to these books. Many of these books are publicly available through libraries. Thus, giving Google rights to these books will essentially privatize libraries. Monopolies reduce the innovation that comes from competition. To allow one company to monopolize the digitization of books will reduce public access to information and inhibit what could be a creative publishing market.

A court in the Southern District of New York will soon make a decision that could determine our digital future.

A ruling is expected shortly on a proposed settlement of lawsuits filed against Google in 2005 by groups representing authors and publishers claiming that Google's book-scanning project violated copyright. When Google announced its project in 2004, the company said its goal was simple yet far-reaching. Like its search engine, which points people to Web sites, Google's book search product would help people find information in books and direct them to volumes in libraries and bookstores.

The project seemed in keeping with the guiding principles of the Internet, which assumes a quid pro quo between search engines and Web sites. That is, sites allow themselves to be copied and indexed as long as search engines such as Google lead people back to the original sites.

But as we learned when the settlement was proposed last October [2008], Google's search tool has become a digital bookstore. The settlement outlines business models for creating and selling electronic editions of books, and selling subscriptions to Google's new exclusive library.

Court-sanctioned Monopolies

Whereas the original lawsuit could have helped define fair use in the digital age, the settlement provides a new and unsettling form of media consolidation.

If approved, the settlement would produce not one but two court-sanctioned monopolies. Google will have permission to bring under its sole control information that has been accessible through public institutions for centuries. In essence, Google will be privatizing our libraries.

Giving control over [broad digital] access to one company, no matter how clever or popular, is a danger to principles we hold dear: free speech, open access to knowledge and universal education.

It may seem puzzling that a civil lawsuit could yield monopolies. Traditionally, class-action lawsuits cluster a group of people who have suffered the same kind of harm as a result of alleged wrongful conduct. And under this settlement, authors who come forward to claim ownership in books scanned by Google would receive $60 per title.

But the settlement would also create a class that includes millions of people who will never come forward. For the majority of books—considered "orphan" works—no one will claim ownership. The author may have died; the publisher might have gone out of business or doesn't respond to inquiries; the original contract has disappeared.

Google would get an explicit, perpetual license to scan and sell access to these in-copyright but out-of-print orphans, which make up an estimated 50 to 70 percent of books published after 1923. No other provider of digital books would enjoy the same legal protection. The settlement also creates a Book Rights Registry that, in conjunction with Google, would set prices for all commercial terms associated with digital books.

Creating a Freely Accessible System

Broad access is the greatest promise or our digital age. Giving control over such access to one company, no matter how clever or popular, is a danger to principles we hold dear: free speech, open access to knowledge and universal education. Throughout history, those principles have been realized in libraries, publishers and legal systems.

The promise of a rich and democratic digital future will be hindered by monopolies.

There are alternatives. Separate from the Google effort, hundreds of libraries, publishers and technology firms are already digitizing books, with the goal of creating an open, freely accessible system for people to discover, borrow, purchase and read millions of titles.

It's not that expensive. For the cost of 60 miles of highway, we can have a 10 million-book digital library available to a generation that is growing up reading on-screen. Our job is to put the best works of humankind within reach of that generation. Through a simple Web search, a student researching the life of John F. Kennedy should be able to find books from many libraries, and many booksellers—and not be limited to one private library whose titles are available for a fee, controlled by a corporation that can dictate what we are allowed to read.

We've wrestled with high-tech monopolies in the past—IBM, AT&T, Microsoft. The lesson was that such strongholds restrict innovation and competition. In those cases, the courts stepped in to address the inequities. Now, we have a proposal for monopolies to be created by the courts.

This settlement should not be approved.[1] The promise of a rich and democratic digital future will be hindered by monopolies. Laws and the free market can support many innovative, open approaches to lending and selling books. We need to focus on legislation to address works that are caught in copyright limbo. And we need to stop monopolies from forming so that we can create vibrant publishing environments.

We are very close to having universal access to all knowledge. Let's not stumble now.

---

1. In March 2011, US Circuit Judge Denny Chin rejected a $125 million settlement of the case, saying it gave Google a "de facto" monopoly to copy books en masse without permission. On May 31, 2012, Chin ruled that authors could sue as a group rather than individually. In August 2012, the 2nd US Circuit Court of Appeals in New York granted Google permission to challenge Chin's May 2012 decision.

8

Large-scale Digitization Projects Will Benefit Writers and Readers

Richard A. Posner

Richard A. Posner is a judge of the US Court of Appeals for the Seventh Circuit and teaches part-time at the University of Chicago Law School. He has written thirty books and more than three hundred articles and book reviews. His academic work since becoming a judge includes studies on intellectual property law.

Although the digitizing of books has had a destructive impact on some bookstores and libraries, according to the economic principle of creative destruction this impact is the price paid for innovation that promotes economic growth. Digital booksellers such as Amazon appear to be profiting the most from the savings that come from more efficient digital publishing practices, but the loss to authors—through piracy, for example—is actually minimal. Copyright laws should be adapted to the revolutionary new ways that content is distributed. Removing copyright restrictions promotes creativity, and all readers would benefit from increased access to the written word. Laws, and private content providers such as Google, must require that users pay at least a small fee for copyrighted work. Moreover, many readers continue to buy printed books.

The great economist Joseph Schumpeter coined the term "creative destruction" to describe the process by which innovation (which might be technological or organizational—the latter illustrated by the invention of the supermarket) promotes economic growth and welfare but at the cost of wiping out existing economic practices or institutions. He thought the process of creative destruction a more important factor in promoting economic welfare than reducing the costs of existing production or improving existing products.

We are seeing creative destruction at work in the information sector because of the digital revolution, which among its other effects has had destructive effects on bookstores and libraries, particularly college and university libraries, now largely unused by students. Amazon is basically a warehousing, order-fulfilling, and delivery agency for books and other consumer products, but the secret of its extraordinary success is that it saves the consumer the bother of going to a bookstore, where he might be quite likely not to find what he's looking for. The bookstore retains only one advantage: browsing is easier in a bookstore than online, although that advantage will diminish as artificial intelligence, which enables Amazon to recommend books to a shopper that the particular shopper might be interested in buying, improves, as it is bound to do.

A New Channel of Distribution

Although Amazon has been devastating for the bookstore industry as a whole, as illustrated by the bankruptcy of Borders, it actually benefits bookstores that specialize in selling out of print books, by marketing the books sold by those bookstores to its customers. But such bookstores account for only a small volume of total book sales.

The Amazon business model, though revolutionary, is visibly in the line of descent from mail-order businesses such as Sears Roebuck. It is a system for the efficient distribution of existing products. The e-book is a new product in one sense, though in another sense it is merely a new channel for distributing the content of books. It is not yet apparent what advantages e-books have over print books except for travelers, other than easier ordering and faster delivery even of printed books from Amazon.

The principal threat that the digital revolution poses to publishers and authors is that of widespread piracy, in violation of copyright law.

Another new product that is also a new channel of distribution is a digitized version of a book that can be read online. This is what has emptied the college and university libraries of their students. Even though copyrighted books are not available in their entirety online, enough such books, along with books that are out of copyright and virtually all academic articles and much other research material as well, are accessible to students online to make a trip to the library unnecessary, except for socializing.

The Digital Threats

We should consider the effect of these revolutionary developments on publishers and especially authors, since the latter are the ultimate creators of the consumption value of books. An improvement in distribution reduces the quality-adjusted cost of the product being distributed, and so should benefit the producer, in this case a combination of the author and the publisher. Amazon, however, appears to have monopsonistic power in the book market, enabling it to capture much of the cost saving from improved distribution. The output of books has not increased during the digital revolution, though this may be due largely to the rise of competing media, fostered by the digital revolution—the enormous variety of information and entertainment, unrelated to books, now available online.

The principal threat that the digital revolution poses to publishers and authors is that of widespread piracy, in violation of copyright law. With the cost of copying and of distributing copied materials having plummeted as a result of the digital revolution, the cost of preventing unauthorized copying and distribution of copied materials has soared. Not that piracy is entirely a bad thing from an author's or publisher's perspective, as it is a kind of advertising—like giving away free samples of a new candy or perfume to excite consumer interest. But if extensive, piracy can substantially diminish an author's earnings.

The importance of copyright, and hence the negative consequences of piracy for the creation of new works, are, however, often exaggerated. Most of the world's great literature was written before the first copyright statute, the Statute of Ann, enacted in 1710. Patronage is an age-old method of remunerating authors, alternative to royalties, and continues to be important: creative writers are hired by colleges, paid by foundations, lecture for money, and sometimes license their work for performance in another medium, such as film or television. Academic publication is largely a patronage system; academics are paid to publish ("publish or perish"). And much creative writing is done not for money but out of a compulsion to write and to be read.

> *Were Google permitted to provide complete online access to all the world's books, in their entirety, the gain in access might more than offset the loss in authors' royalties.*

Copyright law needs to be adapted to the online revolution in distribution. All the books ever published in the world could be digitized—Google has gone far in that direction—and downloaded at no cost. Instead of copyright fees negotiated between author and publisher and therefore dependent on restricting access to the work (and so Google cannot allow access to entire copyrighted works in its vast digital library except to the limited extent permitted by the doctrine of "fair use" or by negotiation with the owners of the copyrights on those works for a copyright license), there could be a modest uniform fee imposed whenever someone, whether a consumer or an e-book publisher, downloaded a book from the Internet. A modest fee would discourage piracy, since piracy requires some technical sophistication and thus is not costless. Printed books would still be bought because most people do not want to read books just online or in an e-book.

An Incomplete Analysis

The standard analysis of the optimal scope of copyright protection holds that it requires a balancing between access (to copyright works) and the incentive to create the works in the first place. But the analysis is incomplete. Access, in a broad sense that allows for copying and not just reading, promotes creativity, because most creative works build on previous works, often improving them by modifications that may be insufficient to avoid liability for copyright infringement. (Think of how Milton's *Paradise Lost* builds on the Adam and Eve story in Genesis.) Obtaining permission to incorporate copyrighted material in a new work can be time consuming, and in the end frustrated by bilateral monopoly problems. And, because copyright terms are now so long (normally 75 years from the death of the author, which may be a century or more after the work was created), it is sometimes impossible to obtain permission to reprint a copyrighted work, simply because the current owner of the copyright cannot be identified.

So, were Google permitted to provide complete online access to all the world's books, in their entirety, the gain in access might more than offset the loss in authors' royalties.

9

A Digital Public Library Will Increase Access to Books for All People

Megan Geuss

Megan Geuss is a staff editor at Ars Technica. *She has also written for other technology-focused publications such as* PCWorld *and* Wired *magazine.*

All citizens deserve access to all of America's library holdings, and a digital public library would provide that access. Developing such a library, however, poses many challenges. For example, some curating of the materials will be necessary, but local libraries will differ on what is offensive or worthless. Scanning all of these materials is a vast undertaking, and a digital public library must be sure that it is not scanning copyrighted materials. One goal is to encourage publishers to allow the library to digitally loan out a few copies of copyrighted books at a time, but digital rights restrictions may stall access to these books. Also difficult will be developing a searchable program interface that will eliminate duplication when combining the data from all libraries. Nevertheless, efforts to develop a digital library will, and should, continue.

Most neighborhoods in America have a public library. Now the biggest neighborhood in America, the Internet, wants a library of its own. Last week [May 2012], *Ars* [*Tech-*

nica] attended a conference held by the Digital Public Library of America, a nascent group of intellectuals hoping to put all of America's library holdings online. The DPLA is still in its infancy—there's no official staff, nor is there a finished website where you can access all the books they imagine will be accessible. But if the small handful of volunteers and directors have their way, you'll see all that by April 2013 at the latest.

Last week's conference set out to answer a lot of questions. How much content should be centralized, and how much should come from local libraries? How will the Digital Public Library be run? Can an endowment-funded public institution succeed where Google Books has largely failed?

Enthusiasm for the project permeated the former Christian Science church where the meeting was held (now the church is the headquarters of Brewster Kahle's Internet Archive). But despite the audience's applause and wide-eyed wonder, there's still a long way to go.

Access to content is crucial to what the DPLA [Digital Public Library of America] is, and much of the usage will be people coming through local libraries.

As it stands, the DPLA has a couple million dollars in funding from charitable trusts like the Alfred P. Sloan Foundation and the Arcadia Fund. The organization is applying for 501(c)3 status this year, and it's not hard to imagine it running as an NPR [National Public Radio]-like entity, with some government funding, some private giving, and a lot of fundraisers. But outside of those details, very little about the Digital Public Library has been decided. "We're still grappling with the fundamental question of what exactly is the DPLA," John Palfrey, chair of the organization's steering committee, admitted. The organization must be a bank of documents, and a vast sea of metadata; an advocate for the people, and a partner with publishing houses; a way to make location irrelevant to library access without giving neighborhoods a reason to cut local library funding. And that will be hard to do.

Real Content, Real Concerns

When people hear "Digital Public Library," many assume a setup like Google Books: a single, searchable hub of books that you can read online, for free. But the DPLA will have to manage expectations on that front. Not only are in-copyright works a huge barrier to entry, but a Digital Public Library will be inextricably tied to local libraries, many of which have their own online collections, often overlapping with other collections.

An online library of America will have to strike a balance between giving centralized marching orders, and acting as an [example] of decentralized cooperation. "On the one hand would [the DPLA only offer] metadata? No, that's not going to be satisfying. Or are we trying to build a colossal database? No that'd be too hard," Palfrey noted to the audience last Friday. "Access to content is crucial to what the DPLA is, and much of the usage will be people coming through local libraries that are using its API [application program interface]. We need something that does change things but doesn't ignore what the Internet is and how it works."

Wikimedia was referenced again and again throughout the conference as a potential model for the library. Could the Digital Public Library act as a decentralized national bookshelf, letting institutions and individuals alike contribute to the database? With the right kind of legal checks, it would certainly make amassing a library easier, and an anything-goes model for the library would bypass arguments over the value of any particular work. Palfrey even suggested to the audience that the DPLA fund "Scan-ebagoes"—Winnebagoes equipped with scanning devices that tour the country and put local area content online.

But the Wikimedia model, where anyone can write or edit entries in the online encyclopedia, could present problems for an organization looking to retain the same credibility as a local library. Several local librarians attended the conference, and voiced concerns over how to incorporate works of local significance and texts published straight to an e-book format, into the national library.

Information should be accessible to anyone who wants it, but some curating might be necessary to make sure every library in America gets on board.

Appraising Content

One member of the audience, who is also a volunteer for the DPLA, suggested in an afternoon presentation that the Library's API incorporate an "up-vote, down-vote" system for works submitted by individuals. You could write a cookbook of Mexican food, he suggested, and if you don't know anything about Mexican food, your book would be down-voted, and in a search it wouldn't show up at the top of the list. A librarian sitting in front of him cautioned that appraising works before they end up in the Digital Public Library is crucial to maintaining its authority—an up-vote, down-vote system could never be enough of a sanity check. "Well if that's true then Reddit wouldn't work," the volunteer shot back. Of course, the trouble is that Reddit *doesn't* work—not like a library, at least, where the voices of women and minorities tend to get shut out in favor of whatever lulz-zeitgeist [funny or interesting cultural, political, or spiritual climate] hit the Internet that morning.

And America is huge: how do you appraise works that may be considered offensive or worthless in some areas (anything from C-list author creationist diatribe, to sex-instructional books with illustrations, to the Anarchist's cookbook)? The easy answer is that all information should be accessible to anyone who wants it, but some curating might be necessary to make sure every library in America gets on board. Although he stipulated that his answer was speculative, Palfrey told *Ars* that individuals would not be contributing to the Digital Public Library, at least at the beginning. "Libraries have done this for a long time, [appraisal] is not a new problem," he said.

Similarly, the Scan-ebago idea is brimming with populist appeal, but Google Books is proof that it's not always as easy as scanning and uploading documents that people want to see online. As a presentation titled "Government, Democracy, and the DPLA," pointed out, even government testimony, while not copyrightable by law, can contain text or images that are copyrightable, like an image of Mickey Mouse, for example. Scanning books is easy, but making sure you have all your legal bases covered before you upload text to the Internet is quite another.

While content is a thorny issue, what the DPLA can leverage to establish itself as a force that won't be ignored by content providers is the massive amount of metadata it's collected about books.

Managing Digital Rights

And how about local book stores and big publishers? They make the content, and some of them will almost certainly try to stonewall this endeavor. But (unsurprisingly) no anti-digital-public-library publishers showed up at the conference that day. Publisher Tim O'Reilly of O'Reilly Media played the print industry's white knight at the DPLA's conference, explaining to the audience how his company adapted to the prevalence of on-demand information. "We've insisted from the beginning that our books be DRM free," he insisted to applause.

Brewster Kahle, another champion of digital (and physical) libraries and the founder of the hosting Internet Archive, suggested that the DPLA buy, say, five electronic copies of an e-book, and digitally lend them out, just like one rents a movie off Amazon or iTunes, which expires in 24 hours or a few days. When an audience member questioned Kahle on what it would take for publishers to nix DRM (or Digital Rights Management restrictions, which confine certain formats to specific e-book readers) for that rent-a-book idea to be more widely viable, Kahle replied facetiously, "Wanting to have a business at the end of the day?"

Kahle and O'Reilly are members of a growing number of publishing industry-types that believe that fixing books to a single e-reader platform is an unsustainable business practice that will naturally become extinct. Their enthusiasm is infectious, but the reality of DRM will certainly be a problem for the Digital Public Library in the short term, if not down the line as well. Wishing DRM away, or convincing charitable investors that it's not going to be a problem, could be an Achilles heel for the Digital Public Library.

Organizing Metadata

While content is a thorny issue, what the DPLA can leverage to establish itself as a force that won't be ignored by content providers is the massive amount of metadata it's collected about books, including data for over 12 million books from Harvard's libraries. These aren't actual books, but details about books you can find in libraries across the country. Sure, it's not exactly a romantic liberation of information, but this data is a roadmap to everything that's available out there, and where users can find it.

Building an API with all of this metadata is also the first step to the ideal because a digital library is useless if search doesn't work. "It's critical to think through search: how to leverage the distributed nature of the internet, and keep [content] in open formats that are linkable," O'Reilly said. With an open API, the organization's extensive database could be distributed to all libraries to build their own digital public library on top of it.

There are other benefits to organizing all the metadata too. Involvement has long been an issue for local libraries, and members of the Digital Public Library's volunteer development team suggested that the API could be used to build social applications on top of the DPLA platform, or map the database and include links to other relevant online databases of culture, like Europeana. "The DPLA could sponsor some research in managing all the metadata," David Weinberger, a member of the DPLA's dev team, suggested. But in the meantime, the group is relying on volunteer time from developers at occasional DPLA-sponsored hackathons.

Citizens deserve a way to access, even just for the duration of a rental, the same ideas that people who live near better-funded libraries can access, without having to engage in piracy.

By April 2013, Weinberger said, the DPLA aims to have a working API with a custom ingestion engine to put metadata from library holdings online, a substantial aggregation of cultural collection metadata and DPLA digitizations, and community developed apps and integration. All mostly from the help of volunteers and open source enthusiasts.

The problem the DPLA has now, explained Weinberger, is figuring out how to build an API that makes use of all the metatdata without giving weight to information that will incorrectly classify a lot of the books. Similarly, he described the DPLA's "deep, deep problem" of "duping" which happens when two caches of data describe the same book differently, leading to duplicates. Weinberger described the "clunky ingestion engine" as "wildly imperfect." If the project is going to get off the ground, it'll need a lot of volunteer help, or a lot of money, and the DPLA is counting on the former, and hoping for the latter.

It Has to Happen, and Fast

"Public education is the most radical idea in the world," Kristina Woolsey, director of San Francisco's Exploratorium, said at last week's conference. "Another radical idea as big as democracy is the idea of public libraries."

Despite the challenges facing the Digital Public Library of America, it's a concept that needs to come to fruition sooner than later. Not simply because a Digital Library would be a professional accomplishment for many well-meaning intellectuals, but because citizens deserve a way to access, even just for the duration of a rental, the same ideas that people who live near better-funded libraries can access, without having to engage in piracy.

One of the earliest speakers at the conference, Dwight McInvaill, a local librarian for North Carolina's Georgetown County Library, spoke of how important it is to digitize works for the good of the public. His own library's digital collection gets over 2 million hits a month. "Small libraries serve 64.7 million people," he said, many of those in poverty. "We must engage forcefully in the bright American Digital Renaissance," McInvaill proclaimed. Either that, or be left in the physical book dark ages.

10

Digitizing Books Will Increase Book Piracy

Scott Turow

Scott Turow is a bestselling American author and a practicing lawyer. He has written numerous novels, including Presumed Innocent, *and two nonfiction books. He is also president of the Authors Guild.*

One of the risks of e-books is piracy. Most authors make little money from writing. The theft of their work further decreases their earnings and threatens a very important part of American culture. The importance of American literary culture is reflected in the US Constitution, which gave Congress the power to create intellectual property laws to inspire innovation and artistic creation. Thus governments must step up efforts to halt book piracy. In addition, publishers must be discouraged from paying lower royalties for e-books; the profits for e-books are actually greater, as there are no costs for paper, printing, warehousing, or distribution. If people value America's literary culture, they will discourage piracy and encourage publishers to pay authors fairly.

Some people argue that books are outmoded, that there are other media available today that offer more immediate methods for delivering knowledge and insight. But right now, long-form, substantively driven, and thoughtful consideration of the challenges that our society is facing and how they must be addressed are served best by this format. Nobody wants to read 250 pages off a computer screen, nor does even the best documentary provide the same opportunity to pause for reflection.

So yes, we will want books. But that doesn't really answer the question of whether evolving commercial conditions will actually support the writing and publication of books.

A confession: I am president of the Authors Guild, the nation's largest membership organization of professional authors. I am trying to protect the livelihoods of American writers, not just because a lot of my friends are authors, but because a vigorous literary culture is an important component of our democracy, not to mention a worthwhile life.

I am not scared of e-books, although I recognize their limitations. E-books don't furnish a room; they don't offer the same reminders, as the presence of a physical book does, of past reading experiences, or the same testimonial to who you are that's silently offered by a book you put on your shelf. But I do most of my book reading these days on an iPad, although I still like to hold broadsheet newspapers in my hands in the morning, and frequently buy hard copies of books I especially like.

Far and away the greatest risk of e-books and e-readers is book piracy.

The Consequences of E-Reading's Popularity

But the increasing popularity of e-books and e-readers has some alarming consequences. The most obvious is that American booksellers, already under heavy pressure from the discounting of bestsellers and online retailing, are being pushed to the point of collapse. Bookstores are not simply places to buy books. They are intellectual hubs in our communities.

My Italian publisher has proposed a model in which bookstores become the place to buy a universal license to own a book in all formats—as a physical object on paper, as an e-book for your reader or computer screen, as an audio book, and whatever else comes down the pipe. But unless momentum gathers quickly for this solution, we will see more and more bookstores going dark.

The second problem is going to be persuading American publishers to maintain a compensation system that maintains reasonable rewards. Right now publishers want to pay a royalty on e-books that is roughly half of what they traditionally paid for books on paper; most are willing to increase that royalty in the second year of a book's life. What the publishers are trying to create is a model that will allow them to recover their costs quickly and to pay less to the authors of books that don't have an extended life.

The problem is that the average American author earns about $9,000 a year from writing as it is. Decreasing the rewards will inevitably drive more people out of the profession. And it is hugely unfair, because publishers do quite well with e-books. They have no costs for paper, printing, warehousing or distribution—and no risk, as is the case with physical books, that the volume will be returned for full credit by the bookseller, which is the great bugaboo of publishing.

The Biggest Threat

But far and away the greatest risk of e-books and e-readers is book piracy. Book pirates, who almost inevitably work offshore, can scan and digitize a new book instantly, which they then offer in any available format at a fraction of the publisher's price. Unchecked, book piracy will destroy the retail book business, much as the illegal swapping of digitized music led to the demise of most retail outlets for popular music. (And please don't tell me about iTunes—authors write whole books that can't be sliced up into segregated units like songs.)

The resulting drop in earnings for authors and publishers and booksellers will wither our literary culture. The Constitution empowered Congress to create intellectual property laws out of a belief that creative monopolies are essential to inspire innovation, which invigorates our society. Wiping out the rewards literally means toppling one of the pillars of our democracy.

Text will live. But we need to think carefully about maintaining the incentives for its creation.

Of course, it is not all doom and gloom. The traditional barriers to becoming an author have been lowered by digitization. The online publication of books, albeit for free, means that first-time authors who can't interest a traditional publisher still have a chance to disseminate their work. I take it for granted that some important new voices will first be heard this way. I like that.

And the promise of digitizing our greatest libraries, so that their contents are available worldwide, will be an enormous boon to freedom of thought everywhere. The legal issues involved are proving difficult in the short run, but I expect those issues to be resolved eventually.

The nonfiction e-book, replete with links to all its sources, to pictures and maps that augment the text, will be a joy. Novels, too, may end up accompanied by some form of instant illustration.

I believe in text and in the uniquely involving experience of reading. And text's efficiency is unrivaled. A picture may be worth a thousand words, but see how many megs those photos absorb on your hard drive, compared to a written description of the same moment. Text will live.

But we need to think carefully about maintaining the incentives for its creation.

11

Digitizing Books Will Not Substantially Increase Book Piracy

Alastair Harper

Alastair Harper is a journalist and a senior policy adviser at Green Alliance, a British environmental think tank, working to ensure that political leaders deliver ambitious solutions to global environmental issues.

The book industry exaggerates the problem of e-book piracy. Indeed, publishers have a vested interest in representing e-book piracy as a significant problem; thus they publish questionable piracy statistics. Research on the types of e-books people actually steal reveals that they are technical or appeal to the prurient interest of adolescents. In truth, few authors, other than those who appeal to a youth audience, show much concern about piracy. In fact, most readers of serious literature continue to prefer physical books. Moreover, publishers who know their history should recall that when some content is made freely available to a broad audience, the result is a greater sale of books.

For years, we have been able to combine our taste for music and film with our desire to stick it to the man, and all from the safety of our PCs. Our literary habits, however, have perforce remained largely legal. The closest we could come to the same thrill is by wearing a deep-pocketed coat to WH

Smiths [a British bookstore]—which is such an analogue approach to theft. Soon, however, even the bookish will be able to frustrate Lord Mandelson[1] because, at long last, thanks to the iPad, digital book piracy is almost upon us.

The surest sign of this is that industry figures have started producing dubious statistics to show how endemic it is. In the US, it's just been announced that 10% of books read are now pirate texts. The same report claims that piracy has cost US publishers $3bn [billion].

But the source of the statistics was a company named Attributor, who provide online piracy protection for the publishing industry. Like a plumber tutting over the state of your pipes, they have a vested interest in finding problems.

Certain juicy targets for piracy . . . have already had their legal battalions ensure no illicit [books] appear online. That the rest of the industry hasn't yet bothered shows how small the impact of piracy has been.

A Limited Impact

A glance at the top seeded ebooks on Pirate Bay shows that [British literary critic and scholar] Christopher Ricks isn't about to lose much sleep over the downloaders. Filling the top slots are Windows 7 Secrets, Adobe CS4 for Photographers and, shamelessly playing up to the stereotype of all geeks being lonely boys, the Jan/Feb edition of *Playboy* magazine. According to Freakbits [a directory of shareable links], the only non-technical or sexual downloaded book in 2009 was the Twilight series—a choice that only goes to show how masturbation and Photoshopping mess with the mind.

More mainstream books are found on Scribd, a site you might well use—it's great for finding free books, citations and

---

1. Lord Peter Mandelson is a member of the House of Lords and an anti-digital-piracy advocate.

excerpts. It's also home to an awful lot of copyright infringements. You can find everything: *Tintin in America*, Martin Amis's *Time's Arrow*, Alastair Campbell's *The Blair Years*, [American satirist] Richard Brautigan. Heck, there's even a bunch of Guardian book bloggers, bundled together in a self-published book of literary quotations.

The interesting thing is just how openly available these books are from the site's servers. In fact, Scribd has a very old-school approach to piracy. It pitches itself as a document-sharing service, just as Napster pitched itself as a way of sharing sound files—a euphemism as transparent as a newspaper ad offering "escorts".

Despite the statistics, I don't believe book piracy will ever be as endemic as it has become with music and film.

Publishers' lawyers will most likely eventually compel Scribd to close, or to turn it into a legal online shop (authors such as Stephen King already sell their digital copies through the site). Certain juicy targets for piracy, such as Stephanie Meyer or JK Rowling, have already had their legal battalions ensure no illicit Potters or vegetarian vampires appear online. That the rest of the industry hasn't yet bothered shows how small the impact of piracy has been on publishers thus far. Faber [a British publisher] clearly don't see the need to police the Alan Bennett plays available on Scribd, since most of their audience still prefer physical copies.

The blog The Millions recently hosted an amazing interview with an American book pirate who provides e-copies of books because of his open-source, anti-copyright beliefs. Dutifully, he scans and proofs every book he uploads. The thought of all that repetitive effort, a kind of digital ironing, is quaintly charming—like a farmer tending to his patch with a sickle, his back squarely turned to the rolling Google combine harvester.

It's such a lot of work and, outside textbooks, it makes so little impact that publishers haven't needed to pay the lawyers' fees to stop it.

A Need to Go Digital

But this is about to change. As e-readers become ubiquitous, publishers know they need to go digital. And being digital, no matter how much drm [digital rights management] you shove in, means content will be pirated. Anyone will be able to get any new book you want if you know how to look for it.

But, despite the statistics, I don't believe book piracy will ever be as endemic as it has become with music and film. We've moved on from the pre-iTunes days when the only way of getting an MP3 of a song was to find it on Napster. Publishers were keen to get on board with the iPad straight from launch because they knew it was the safest way to protect and to disseminate their product. One editor at a big publisher told me just how desperate his company have been to woo Apple over the last 18 months.

More importantly, though, publishers have a headstart on the music and film industries and already have some experience of what happens when controlled content is made widely available for free. Victorian publishers were convinced public libraries would ruin them: they didn't. Lending libraries brought books off the estates and into the tenements, and publishers were suddenly selling a lot more books to a lot more people. This happened as the result of a system that, like Spotify, allowed readers to legally obtain books for free while the authors still received some money. If the publishing industry can remember its own history, digitisation should be a doddle.

12

E-books Are an Environmentally Friendly Option

Julia Silverman

Julia Silverman is a writer living in Portland, Oregon, who writes on environmental and child-care issues.

The production of both electronic and print books yields carbon emissions that threaten the environment. However, transporting printed books uses more carbon-producing energy. Moreover, publishers destroy unsold print books and many others end up in landfills. Thus, environmentally conscious citizens who are also avid readers should consider the e-reader. Unfortunately, some consumers replace their e-readers with the latest model before the older models reach the end of their useful life. If improperly disposed of, these readers produce toxic waste that pollutes waterways. Nevertheless, for those readers who keep their e-readers for many years, e-books are a sensible environmental alternative.

The e-mail from Multnomah County Library finally arrived, informing me it was finally my turn for the book I'd awaited for months. Turns out, I couldn't wait that long to read "The Paris Wife," Paula McLain's absorbing tale of Ernest Hemingway's plain Jane first wife. I'd downloaded it on my shiny new iPad 2 months earlier.

The American Academy of Publishers projects that e-books will account for 25 percent of all book sales in a few years, and 75 percent by 2025. A new Pew Research report says about 12 percent of Americans own some kind of e-reader. Already, insanely expensive textbooks are being phased out, replaced by online-only versions. *The New York Times* now has a bestseller list just for e-books.

What's it mean for the environment, and the sustainably conscious book-lover?

The answer is as layered as anything William Faulkner ever dreamed up.

It takes purchasing about 40 to 50 new paperbound books to equal the cost of fossil fuels, mineral consumption and water use of a single e-reader.

Manufacturing Requirements

Traditional books require deforestation, though the industry has made significant strides in producing books from recycled materials and soy-based inks. Minerals and other materials needed to produce an iPad, Kindle or Nook are more problematic. Raz Godelnik, the chief executive of EcoLibris, a nonprofit that focuses on sustainability in publishing, says some of the minerals needed to make electronic gadgets come from ravaged regions like the Democratic Republic of the Congo, and profits have gone into local civil war efforts, giving e-readers a significant social toll.

Production of both types of books causes carbon emissions, though books require more energy for transporting from publisher to bookstore.

Daniel Goleman, a behavioral researcher, has calculated that overall, it takes purchasing about 40 to 50 new paperbound books to equal the cost of fossil fuels, mineral consumption and water use of a single e-reader. Consider global warming contributions, and that number goes up to about 100 books, Goleman figures.

Verdict: If you're a serious reader, the electronic reader is the way to go, so long as you hang onto it for a few years.

The Versatility Question

Let's say you buy a book, read it and love it. Then what? You can pass it on to a friend, keep it on your shelf to read again someday, donate it, or try to sell it back to one of Portland's many used-book stores.

My new iPad stores a whole bunch of books in my virtual library, and I use it to read *The New York Times*, *The New Yorker* and *People* magazine. I can get rid of my dead-tree subscriptions to these publications, pay digitally to read them and not miss a beat. The iPad is also a phone book, a music player, a calendar and a photo album.

Verdict: The iPad wins this one hands down.

The Cost of Print and E-Books

The price of e-readers has dropped steadily. Kindles are now available for as little as $114, or less than buying six hardcover books brand-new. Multi-use iPads are much more expensive, starting at a splurge-but-not-out-of-the-question $499.

Of course, you can get all the books you want—eventually—for free at your local library. Once you've gotten your reader, plenty of classic books are available for free as well.

Given the lack of overhead, individual e-books cost less than their new hardback versions. The nearly 800-page tome by local author Jean Auel, "Land of the Painted Caves," lists for $30, but it's available as an e-book for $12.99.

Verdict: Books, for those who rely on the library. If you're a voracious reader who absolutely has to dive into the new Jonathan Franzen the day it comes out, get an e-reader.

Weighing the Waste Options

Plenty of books do end up in landfills. And a staggering 30 percent or so of new books will, on average, fail to sell and be shipped back to their publisher's warehouse to be destroyed. On the other hand, Apple cranked out the iPad 2 a mere year after introducing its prototype iPad, and new versions of the Kindle and Nook have emerged quickly. Plenty of consumers are happy to chuck their old electronic device for the newer, glitzier version, and that can mean growing amounts of e-waste.

E-recycling is getting easier. But old computers and e-readers can wind up overseas, being stripped for metal parts, exposing toxins and polluting waterways.

Verdict: A toss-up, for now.

Local Impact

The e-book revolution is a big part of why so many local bookstores have closed their doors in recent years.

But e-books are extraordinarily democratizing. Maybe your next-door neighbor is a secret genius, but has never been able to get a big-name publisher to look her way. There's limitless room in the e-bookstores of the world for authors of all stripes. And the returns can be decent. While a published author may see returns of 15 percent to 20 percent on a traditional book, e-books can net authors up to 70 percent returns.

For those who always want a new book at their bedside, and who plan to hang onto their device for a few years, an e-reader looks like a reasonable environmental choice.

Powell's Books is trying to satisfy both sides of the coin, says Darin Sennett, director of strategic projects. Shoppers can now download e-books via the Powell's website thanks to a partnership with Google e-books. In a few months, he says, shoppers will be able to buy either a paper or electronic edition of the book they've chosen, on the spot.

Powell's can compete with the big-name e-book sellers, he says, because of its curated choices and customer service.

E-Readers Can Benefit the Reader and the Environment

The most environmentally friendly bookworms are those who walk or bike to their local library to get their book fix. But e-readers have more people reading, because of the immediacy and accessibility of the medium. And that can only be a good thing.

For those who always want a new book at their bedside, and who plan to hang onto their device for a few years, an e-reader looks like a reasonable environmental choice.

13

E-books Are Not Better for the Environment than Print Books

Nick Moran

Nick Moran is the social media editor for The Millions, *an on-line magazine offering coverage on books, arts, and culture. He previously worked for Norton, John Wiley & Sons, and Oxford University Press.*

Those who claim that reading books electronically is better for the environment than reading print books often provide mislead-ing data. The claim that reading e-books produces fewer carbon emissions does not account for the lifetime use of the e-reader, which actually produces five times the carbon emissions in one year of average reading. Although the e-reader's carbon footprint does equal that of print books over five years, in truth, most people replace their e-readers every two years. Thus, e-readers can produce a carbon footprint 250 percent greater than that of print books. Moreover, improperly discarded e-readers create dangerous electronic waste. Both print and e-books pose a threat to the environment; the truly environmentally conscious reader should borrow books from the library.

In 2009, the Book Industry Environmental Council set a couple of environmental goals for the U.S. book industry. Using a calculation of the industry's total greenhouse gas emissions from 2006 as its baseline, the BIEC and its members pledged to reduce the industry's carbon footprint by 20% in 2020 and by 80% in 2050. When the pledge was made, the Kindle had existed for only a year and a half, and the Nook was still eight months away. (Kobo eReaders and iPads didn't emerge until 2010.) eBooks, still in their infancy, accounted for a measly 5% of books sold in America.

Today, it seems like many publishing houses are on their ways toward achieving the BIEC goals. Thanks to the proliferation of FTP [File Transfer Protocol] software, most major publishing houses have slashed the amount of printing done in-office. At John Wiley & Sons, my production group had a paperless workflow: Adobe was our editing tool of choice, and to be one of our freelancers, you had to pass an exhaustive MS Word screening test. Later on, at Oxford University Press, a common email signature asked readers to "save paper and print only what's necessary." Organizing stacks of paper on your desk was out; navigating sub-folders on a shared drive was in.

The Growth of eBooks

Meanwhile eBooks were becoming ever more popular. By the end of 2011, Amazon announced it was selling one million Kindles a week, and Apple said it had sold over 40 million iPads. Consequently, eBooks accounted for 31% of U.S. book sales by 2012. According to a Pew Internet study, as many as one in four American adults now own an eReader or tablet (one in three if they went to college). The trend toward digitization is undeniable, and there are many reasons to be optimistic: big publishers are making more money off of more products than ever before; it's easier than ever to publish a book; and the number of books available to anyone with an internet connection is unprecedented. Some analysts even predict that soon print books, like CDs a few years ago, will be almost entirely replaced by digital files.

But is all of this really cutting the industry's carbon footprint? Is total eBook adoption—that is: elimination of the print book—really an ecologically responsible goal?

Put in absolute terms, the number of books—regardless of format—produced and sold across the globe increases each year. This is mostly due to an increasing global population. While America, Australia, India and the UK are the most rapid adopters of digital reading devices—at least for the time being—eBooks presently account for only a small fraction of the world book market. (This is due to factors such as availability of technology, reliable internet connections, and disposable income.)

Necessarily, the increased consumption of print and digital books has led to an ever-increasing demand for the materials required to create, transport, and store them. In the case of eBooks, though, vast amounts of materials are also necessary for the eReaders themselves, and this is something typically overlooked by proponents of digitization: the material costs are either ignored, or, more misleadingly, they're classified as the byproduct of the tech industry instead of the book industry.

Vast amounts of materials are . . . necessary for the eReaders themselves, and this is something typically overlooked by proponents of digitization.

Compounding the Carbon Footprint

National Geographic correspondent Allen Tellis recently posted a brief note of encouragement to owners of eReaders, and it illustrates exactly the type of oversight I just mentioned. "The steady rise of eBooks," Tellis wrote, "should benefit the environment by reducing use of paper and ink, and by slashing transportation, warehouse, and shelf-space limits." He went on to note how certain study groups have determined "that the carbon released from eBooks is offset after people read more than 14 eBooks" on a single eReader. But Tellis ignores the fact that global print book consumption is rising concurrently with eBook consumption. In other words: the carbon footprint of the digital book industry is mostly growing *in addition to*, not to the detriment of, the growing carbon footprint of the print book industry.

I couldn't locate the source of Tellis' information about those 14 eBooks offsetting the ecological cost of their owner's eReader. Instead, I found this *New York Times* op-ed which painted a starkly different picture: "the impact of one e-reader . . . equals roughly 40 to 50 books. When it comes to global warming, though, it's 100 books." Still more damning, Ted Genoways' excellent *VQR* [*Virginia Quarterly Review*] article about the raw materials needed for the production of eReaders (and other gizmos), found that:

> At present, the average e-reader is used less than two years before it is replaced. That means that the nearly ten million e-readers expected to be in use by next year would have to supplant the sales of 250 million new books—not used or rare editions, 250 million new books—each year just to come out footprint-neutral. Considering the fact that the Association of American Publishers estimates that the combined sales of all books in America (adult books, children's books, textbooks, and religious works) amounted to fewer than 25 million copies last year, we have already increased the environmental impact of reading by tenfold. Moreover, it takes almost exactly fifty times as much fossil fuel production to power an iPad for the hours it takes to read a book as it would take to read the same book on paper by electric light.

A Misleading Comparison

Usage figures are an important element in the estimation of a book's environmental impact. According to Apple, an iPad is responsible for 2.5 grams of CO_{2e} per hour of use. A single print book, on the other hand, is responsible for "a net 8.85 pounds" (PDF) of carbon emissions over the course of its life (e.g. production, transportation, and retail). Note that the former figure, however, is open-ended; the latter figure is finite. If you ignore the environmental cost of an eReader, that means you would need to read the iBookstore version of *War and Peace* for 1,605.39 hours (˜67 days) to damage the environment as badly as that paperback copy of Tolstoy's tome on your bookshelf. That certainly sounds like a point for eBooks, but it's a totally misleading evaluation.

For a demonstration of just how misleading that comparison is, I used basic arithmetic and some minimal Googling to calculate the carbon footprint of the *average* American reading an *average* number of *average* novels at an *average* speed both in print and on an iPad. (I picked iPads because Amazon doesn't release Kindle data. I picked America because we're the most voracious consumers of digital books.) Here's what I found:

One Year of Reading: First I calculated the average rate of consumption for the average reader. I found average reading speed, average book length, and average number of books consumed, and then I calculated the carbon emissions caused by one year of reading.

1. The average adult reads 200–250 words per minute.

2. The average novel is 64,500 words.

3. That means the average adult spends 4.3 hours reading an average novel. [(64,500 words / 250 wpm) / 60 minutes]

4. The average adult reads 6.5 books per year.

5. The average adult spends 27.95 hours reading each year. [6.5 books x 4.3 hours]

Paperback Footprint: 26,087.59 grams of CO_{2e} [6.5 books x 8.85 pounds of emissions x 453.5 g. per lb.]

eBook Footprint: 69.875 grams of CO_{2e} [6.5 books x 4.3 hours x 2.5 g. of emissions per hr.]

This is the comparison eBook proponents typically cite. Unfortunately, it's at best lousy mathematics and at worst a manipulative comparison.

One year of reading eBooks accounts for a carbon footprint five times greater than a year's worth of print books.

One Year of Reading (Device Footprints Included): Next I found the lifetime carbon emissions from one iPad and one iPad 2, and I plugged those into my one year of reading calculations.

iPad lifetime emissions: 130,000 grams of CO_{2e}

iPad 2 lifetime emissions: 105,000 grams of CO_{2e}

Paperback Footprint: 26,087.59 grams of CO_{2e}

eBook Footprint (iPad): 130,069.875 grams of CO_{2e}

eBook Footprint (iPad 2): 105,069.875 grams of CO_{2e}

As you can plainly see, factoring in the carbon footprint of an eReader drastically changes the comparison. One year of reading eBooks accounts for a carbon footprint five times greater than a year's worth of print books.

Fans of eReaders will of course refute this data by claiming that their devices level out with—and could even become "greener" than—print books on a long enough timeline. This claim *is* indeed theoretically true after five years, and I'll show you how.

Five Years of Reading on One Device (Device Footprints Included): I extrapolated the data to account for five years of use at the same rate of consumption as above. (And on the same device for all five years—more on that in a minute.)

Paperback Footprint: 130,437.95 grams of CO_{2e}

eBook Footprint (iPad): 130,349.375 grams of CO_{2e}

eBook Footprint (iPad 2): 105,349.375 grams of CO_{2e}

I determined that it takes five years (32.5 books) of steady ebook consumption (on the same device) to match the ecological footprint of reading the same number of print books the old fashioned way. This number is smack in between Tellis' (14 books) and *New York Times*' (50 books) calculations. However it, too, is misleading because it doesn't correctly account for device replacement.

As Ted Genoways was saying, most eReaders are used for only two years before being discarded, replaced, lost or broken. More than 20% of all Kindles sit unused after Christmas. So, that in mind, let's look at the numbers when we factor in average eReader use—and account for device replacement every two years.

Five Years of Reading (Device Replacement Included): Assuming a device is replaced every two years (years 0, 2, and 4) . . . [the eReader] accounts for an initial carbon footprint 200–250% greater than your typical household library, and it increases every time you get a new eReader for Christmas, or every time the latest Apple Keynote lights a fire in your wallet.

Outdated devices are too often discarded inappropriately. You don't need to investigate very hard to find evidence of the toll this mineral mining and e-waste dumping takes on fragile ecosystems.

Also, these figures simply calculate the impact one person's consumption has on the environment. If you live in a household with multiple eReaders—say, one for your husband and one for your daughter, too—your family's carbon emissions are more than 600–750% higher per year than they would be if you invested in a bunch of bookshelves or, better yet, a library card.

Complicating Factors

Things are trickier than they seem, too. The truth is that the dedicated eReader died almost as soon as it arrived, and it's since been replaced by items even worse for the environment than its ancestors. What we presently refer to as eReaders are more like all-purpose tablets equipped with email clients, web browsers, games, movie players, and more. (Even one of the earliest generations of Kindles offered a prototype web browser—buried in subfolders within the device's navigation system, though clearly a hint of what was coming.) As these devices become more sophisticated, they invite more prolonged usage, so those 2.5 g of emissions per hour of use continue to add up. Likewise, as these devices become more sophisticated, their manufacture demands more precious materials—often from Southeast Asia, Africa, and South America.

Still more problematic is the fact that outdated devices are too often discarded inappropriately. You don't need to investigate very hard to find evidence of the toll this mineral mining and e-waste dumping takes on fragile ecosystems.

The emissions and e-waste numbers could be stretched even further if I went down the resource rabbit hole to factor in: electricity needed at the Amazon and Apple data centers; communication infrastructure needed to transmit digital files across vast distances; the incessant need to recharge or replace the batteries of eReaders; the resources needed to recycle a digital device (compared to how easy it is to pulp or recycle a book); the packaging and physical mailing of digital devices; the need to replace a device when it breaks (instead of replacing a book when it's lost); the fact that every reader of eBooks requires his or her own eReading device (whereas print books can be loaned out as needed from a library); the fact that most digital devices are manufactured abroad (and therefore transported across oceans); and etc. . . .

This is the ultimate result of our culture's fetishization of technology—a problem which will assuredly worsen before it improves. It wasn't long ago that sophisticated electronics were few and far between. I grew up in a house with one desktop computer, and it was located in the kitchen. That was eleven years ago, and when I remember all the times I argued with my brother over who got to play StarCraft, my memory seems as quaint and outdated as a scene from *Mad Men*. Today, my thirteen-year-old sister has her own laptop, smartphone, and television to supplement the two desktop computers, additional television set, and Kindle Fire located in my mother's home.

There's an Apple store in Grand Central Station that I pass each day on my way to work; every morning I watch hundreds of commuters browse iPads as though they were magazines or candy. In the end, this conspicuous (and often unnecessary) tech consumption—eReaders included—contributes to an inflating carbon footprint far beyond anything ever caused by traditional book production.

> *The responsible decision is to purchase or borrow books printed on recycled paper and from ecologically conscious vendors.*

Addressing the Carbon Footprint of Both Industries

Of course, it's slippery ethics to rationalize the book industry's carbon footprint by focusing, instead, on the larger problem of the tech industry's carbon footprint. Both are problems that need to be addressed. But for right now, if we're forced to choose, the traditional paper route is the better one. If you worry for the future of our rainforests, and if you worry for the future of our planet, the responsible decision is to purchase or borrow books printed on recycled paper and from ecologically conscious vendors. . . .

While this tactic alone will not solve the problem, it will certainly make a difference if enough people choose library cards instead of Kindle Singles. And while it's true that, now that digital has arrived, digital is here to stay, the book reading community needs to ask itself which is more important: developing a greener way to produce print books while we halt the growth of eBooks' market share, committing fully to the creation of "greener" eReading devices—or some combination of both. Doing neither is not an option.

14

Colleges Should Mandate That All Textbooks Be Digitized

Marc Prensky

Marc Prensky is a software designer and author of Teaching Digital Natives: Partnering for Real Learning *and* From Digital Natives to Digital Wisdom.

Colleges and universities should ban nonelectronic books to improve the way faculty teach and students learn. A print textbook ban will not discourage reading, nor diminish the value of the ideas within books. In fact, e-books liberate ideas. Faculty can augment texts with additional multimedia materials that enhance the content. Moreover, faculty can expand e-text discussion to students outside the classroom, enriching the educational experience. Digital texts are also accessible anywhere, at any time, while printed books, once read, are often closed and shelved. Electronic textbooks free ideas from the printed page and will move education into the twenty-first century.

Recent news that South Korea plans to digitize its entire elementary- and secondary-school curriculum by 2015, combined with the declining cost of e-readers and Amazon's announcement earlier this year [2011] that it is selling more e-books than print books, prompts an interesting question: Which traditional campus will be the first to go entirely bookless? Not, of course, bookless in the sense of using no book content, but bookless in the sense of allowing no physical books. My guess is that this will make some institution famous.

Already, just about everything that an undergraduate needs to read is available in electronic form. Whatever isn't there electronically, librarians, students, or professors can easily scan, as many already do.

A Bookless College

Some colleges are already heading in this direction by requiring or handing out iPod Touches, iPads, Kindles, or Nooks, often preloaded with textbooks and other curricular materials, or by disallowing paper texts for online courses. But I suggest that it's time to go much further: to actually ban nonelectronic books on campus. That would be a symbolic step toward a much better way of teaching and learning, in which all materials are fully integrated. It could involve a pledge similar to the one that language students and instructors at Middlebury Language Schools take to speak only the foreign languages in which they are immersed during the study program.

> I'm not advocating that we get rid of the good and valuable ideas, thoughts, or words in books—only that we transfer them to (and have students absorb them through) another form.

In this bookless college, all reading—which would still, of course, be both required and encouraged—would be done electronically. Any physical books in students' possession at the beginning of the year would be exchanged for electronic versions, and if a student was later found with a physical book, it would be confiscated (in return for an electronic version). The physical books would be sent to places and institutions that wanted or needed them. Professors would have a limited time in which to convert their personal libraries to all-digital formats, using student helpers who would also record the professors' marginal notes.

Moving Education Into the Future

Why, in a world in which choice and personal preference are highly valued, would any college want to create such a mandate? Because it makes a bold statement about the importance of moving education into the future. It is, in a sense, only a step removed from saying, "We no longer accept theses on scrolls, papyrus, or clay tablets. Those artifacts do still exist in the world, but they are not the tools of this institution." Or: "In this institution we have abandoned the slide rule. Those who find it useful and/or comforting can, of course, use it, but not here."

Let me be clear that I'm not advocating that we get rid of the good and valuable ideas, thoughts, or words in books— only that we transfer them to (and have students absorb them through) another form. Much of what students need to study is already in the public domain and can easily, in instances where it hasn't already been done, be converted to electronic form. Most contemporary works exist electronically, as do a huge number of historical books and documents. This would be an incentive to scan more of them. It would also provide an opportunity for academics and others to consider how notions of intellectual-property rights might need to be updated for the digital age.

Addressing the Pushback

Of course, pushback is to be expected. I think less of it would come from faculties in the sciences, who feel most deeply the need to connect information more completely and be sure it is up-to-date, than from humanities faculties, who often teach particular physical books (and might tend to be far more attached to them). Such a mandate might not go over well with all students, either, at least at first, because many have been inculcated since birth to appreciate the value of physical books.

But I believe the change would be transformational, in very positive ways, for education. Once the change happened, the college and its professors would be expected to enhance all electronic texts in useful ways. Student materials might contain not just the commentary of the individual professor but of professors all over the world. A student's *Hamlet* might contain not just the notes that a student would find in a print edition but collective notes from actors, directors, scholars, and other contributors. The college's version of *Hamlet* might be linked to whatever notes Laurence Olivier or Harold Bloom had written in the margins of their own copies. It might be linked to scenes and versions already on YouTube, or to open courseware from institutions around the world.

Curating Enhancement

Selecting and curating such enhancements to enlighten students without overwhelming them would be the responsibility of the professors. They could build in questions that would prompt reflection and discussion, and have those discussions shared classwide, campuswide, or worldwide. Students could keep online records of all their notes, thoughts, and readings; and, unlike with traditional college texts, they could find, collate, and link to those notes and records forever.

Many entrepreneurs are already inventing software that allows the quick and fertile connection of one's ideas and those of others, but an all-digital campus would provide a powerful incentive to develop those programs even faster and take them further. Various all-digital campuses could collaborate to develop specifications for such helpful software as well as open-source tools.

The Advantages of an All-Digital Campus

Sure, it will take some transition time to get to the all-digital college, but the advantages are many.

First, we would wean students (and scholars) off the physical books of the past, just as they were once weaned off scrolls when new and more efficient technology came along. I have heard all the arguments for the physical book, from the "feel of the page" to the effects of "printed vs. on-screen words" to the "way we take in information" to the fact that "a book lasts a long time." But those arguments are unconvincing when weighed against the many advantages of going all-electronic. Far better than having colleges preserve the use of physical books for certain advantages would be for colleges to find ways to ensure that we can achieve all the results we want with the integrated tools of the future.

The physical book is, in many ways, a jail for ideas— once a book is read, closed, and shelved, for most people it tends to stay that way.

Second, books—and commentaries on books—would start to be connected in ways they aren't now. We could actually search for the source of a particular quote, or for comments on particular ideas and passages, in ways we can't even begin to do today. Yet the integrity of the individual work would still be preserved.

Third, and I believe this to be the greatest advantage, ideas would be freed from the printed page, where they have been held captive for too many centuries. In addition to being a dissemination mechanism and an archive, the physical book is, in many ways, a jail for ideas—once a book is read, closed, and shelved, for most people it tends to stay that way. Many of us have walls lined with books that will never be reopened, most of what is in them long forgotten.

But what if all those books were in our pockets and could be referred to whenever we thought of them? The idea of having one's own personal library of physical books, so useful in earlier times, is no longer worth passing on to our students;

the idea of building a digital pocket library of books that students could visit and revisit at any time certainly is.

Liberating Ideas

Colleges and professors exist, in great measure, to help "liberate" and connect the knowledge and ideas in books. We should certainly pass on to our students the ability to do this. But in the future those liberated ideas—the ones in the books (the author's words), and the ones about the books (the reader's own notes, all readers' thoughts and commentaries)—should be available with a few keystrokes. So, as counterintuitive as it may sound, eliminating physical books from college campuses would be a positive step for our 21st-century students, and, I believe, for 21st-century scholarship as well. Academics, researchers, and particularly teachers need to move to the tools of the future. Artifacts belong in museums, not in our institutions of higher learning.

So will your campus be the first to go bookless? It's a risky step, certainly, but one that will attract forward-thinking students and professors, and be long remembered.

Organizations to Contact

The editors have compiled the following list of organizations concerned with the issues debated in this book. The descriptions are derived from materials provided by the organizations. All have publications or information available for interested readers. The list was compiled on the date of publication of the present volume; the information provied here may change. Be aware that many organizations take several weeks or longer to respond to inquiries, so allow as much time as possible.

American Library Association (ALA)
50 E. Huron St., Chicago, IL   60611
(800) 545-2433
website: www.ala.org

The American Library Association (ALA) was founded in 1896 to help develop, promote, and improve libraries in the United States with the goal of enhancing learning and ensuring access to information for all. The ALA publishes a number of periodicals, including *American Libraries, Booklist*, and *Library Technology Reports*. The association also publishes articles on the impact of digitizing books, some of which are available on its website.

Association of American Publishers (AAP)
455 Massachusetts Ave. NW, Suite 700
Washington, DC   20001-2777
(202) 347-3375 • fax: (202) 347-3690
website: www.publishers.org

The Association of American Publishers (AAP) is a trade association for US book publishers. It represents the industry's interests on policy, legislation, and regulatory issues. These interests include the protection of intellectual property rights and worldwide copyright enforcement, digital and new technology issues, funding for education and libraries, tax and trade, censorship, and literacy. Resources available on the AAP website include the following report: *The Rise in E-Reading*.

The Authors Guild

31 East 32nd St., 7th Floor, New York, NY   10016
(212) 564-5904 • fax: (212) 564-5363
e-mail: staff@authorsguild.org
website: www.authorsguild.org

Founded as the Authors League of America in 1912, the guild is the nation's leading advocate for writers' interests in effective copyright protection, fair contracts, and free expression. The *Authors Guild Bulletin* is a quarterly review covering the latest in publishing, copyright, tax, legal, and legislative news and offers essential information for published writers. Articles on the Google book digitization lawsuit are available on its website.

Berkman Center for Internet & Society

Harvard University, 23 Everett St., 2nd Floor
Cambridge, MA   02138
(617) 495-7547 • fax: (617) 495-7641
e-mail: cyber@law.harvard.edu
website: http://cyber.law.harvard.edu

The Berkman Center for Internet & Society was founded to explore cyberspace, share in its research, and help pioneer its development. The center explores a wide spectrum of Internet issues, including governance, privacy, intellectual property, antitrust, content control, and electronic commerce. The Berkman Center will convene a large and diverse group of stakeholders to define the scope, architecture, costs, and administration for a proposed Digital Public Library of America. The committee plans to bring together representatives from the educational community, public and research libraries, cultural organizations, state and local government, publishers, authors, and private industry in a series of meetings and workshops to examine strategies for improving public access to comprehensive online resources. Information on this project is available on its website.

Creative Commons (CC)
171 Second St., Suite 300, San Francisco, CA   94105
(415) 369-8480 • fax: (415) 278-9419
website: http://creativecommons.org

Creative Commons (CC) is a nonprofit licensing organization, seeking to make creative works free for certain uses. Like the free software and open-source movements, CC's ends are cooperative and community-minded, but its means are voluntary and libertarian. The organization works to offer creators protection for their works while encouraging certain uses of them.

Independent Book Publishers Association (IBPA)
1020 Manhattan Beach Blvd., Suite 204
Manhattan Beach, CA   90266
(310) 546-1818 • fax: (310) 546-3939
e-mail: info@IBPA-online.org
website: www.ibpa-online.org

The Independent Book Publishers Association (IBPA) is a nonprofit trade association representing independent book publishers in the United States and around the world. The association seeks to advance the professional interests of independent publishers by providing cooperative marketing programs, education, and advocacy within the publishing industry. The IBPA offers members access to articles on e-book publishing, including "Save Time and Money by Designing with E-books in Mind," "E-book Conversions: Ten Pointers to Ensure Reader Enjoyment (and Minimize E-book Returns)," and "E-book Reality Show (and Tell)."

Institute for the Future of the Book
74 N. 7th St. #3, Brooklyn, New York   11211
website: www.futureofthebook.org

The Institute for the Future of the Book is a think tank that experiments with future forms of the book. Because the institute believes that the printed page is giving way to the networked screen, its mission is to chronicle this shift and impact its development in a positive direction. The institute is a project of the Annenberg Center for Communication at the University of Southern California and is based in Brooklyn, New York. The institute's if:book blog, which is available on its website, covers a wide range of concerns, all in some way fitting into the "techno-cultural puzzle that is the future of ideas." Bloggers on if:book also build open source software and lead publishing experiments with authors, academics, artists, and programmers.

Novelists, Inc. (Ninc)
PO Box 2037, Manhattan, KS   66505
fax: (785) 537-1877
e-mail: ninc@varney.com
website: www.ninc.com

Novelists, Inc. (Ninc) is an organization that promotes the creative contributions of novelists and their rights to be treated with dignity, to be recognized as the sole owners of their literary creations, and to be fairly compensated for their writings. Ninc publishes a blog, a newsletter, and various other publications, including *A Comprehensive Guide to the New World of Publishing* and *The Future of Publishing*.

Pew Internet & American Life Project
1615 L St. NW, Suite 700, Washington, DC   20036
(202) 419-4500 • (202) 419-4505
website: www.pewinternet.org

The Pew Internet & American Life Project is one of seven projects that make up the Pew Research Center, a nonpartisan, nonprofit "fact tank" that provides information on the issues, attitudes, and trends shaping America and the world. The project produces reports exploring the impact of the Internet and digital media on families, communities, work and home, daily life, education, health care, and civic and political life.

Project Gutenberg Literary Archive Foundation
809 North 1500 West, Salt Lake City, UT   84116
website: www.gutenberg.org

Project Gutenberg is a collection of free e-books created by Michael Hart, credited as the inventor of e-books. The project's mission is to encourage the creation and distribution of e-books, and help give them away. The website has a search engine that offers various ways to browse and select free e-books.

World Intellectual Property Organization (WIPO)
PO Box 18, Geneva 20   CH-1211
 Switzerland
+41 22 338 9111 • fax: +41 22 733 5428
website: www.wipo.int

The World Intellectual Property Organization (WIPO) is a specialized agency of the United Nations. It is dedicated to developing a balanced and accessible international intellectual property system. WIPO was established by the WIPO Convention in 1967 with a mandate from its member states to promote the protection of intellectual property throughout the world through cooperation among states and in collaboration with other international organizations.

Bibliography

Books

Chris Anderson *Free: The Future of a Radical Price.* New York: Hyperion, 2009.

Mark Bauerlein *The Dumbest Generation: How the Digital Age Stupefies Young Americans and Jeopardizes Our Future.* New York: Jeremy P. Tarcher/Penguin, 2008.

John Brockman *Is the Internet Changing the Way You Think? The Net's Impact on Our Minds and Future.* New York: HarperCollins, 2011.

Allan Collins and Richard Halverson *Rethinking Education in the Age of Technology: The Digital Revolution and Schooling in America.* New York: Teachers College Press, 2009.

Robert Darnton *The Case for Books: Past, Present, and Future.* New York: Public Affairs, 2009.

George Dyson *Turing's Cathedral: The Origins of the Digital Universe.* New York: Pantheon, 2012.

Jeff Gomez *Print Is Dead: Books in Our Digital Age.* New York: Macmillan, 2008.

N. Katherine Hayles *How We Think: Digital Media and Contemporary Technogenesis.* Chicago: University of Chicago Press, 2012.

Maggie Jackson	*Distracted: The Erosion of Attention and the Coming Dark Age.* New York: Prometheus, 2008.
Alan Jacobs	*The Pleasures of Reading in an Age of Distraction.* New York: Oxford University Press, 2011.
Marilyn Johnson	*This Book Is Overdue! How Librarians and Cybrarians Can Save Us All.* New York: HarperCollins, 2010.
Andrew Keen	*The Cult of the Amateur: How Blogs, MySpace, YouTube, and the Rest of Today's User-Generated Media Are Destroying Our Economy, Our Culture, and Our Values.* New York: Doubleday, 2009.
Rebecca MacKinnon	*Consent of the Networked: The World-wide Struggle for Internet Freedom.* New York: Basic Books, 2012.
William J. Martin	*Books, Bytes, and Business: The Promise of Digital Publishing.* Burlington, VT: Ashgate, 2010.
Roger McHaney	*The New Digital Shoreline: How Web 2.0 and Millennials Are Revolutionizing Higher Education.* Sterling, VA: Stylus, 2011.
James Mussell	*The Nineteenth-Century Press in the Digital Age.* Hampshire, UK: Palgrave Macmillan, 2012.

John G. Palfrey and Urs Gasser — *Born Digital: Understanding the First Generation of Digital Natives.* New York: Basic Books, 2008.

Thomas Pfeffer — *Virtualization of Universities: Digital Media and the Organization of Higher Education Institutions.* New York: Springer, 2012.

Marc Prensky — *From Digital Natives to Digital Wisdom: Hopeful Essays for 21st Century Learning.* Thousand Oaks, CA: Corwin, 2012.

Marc Prensky — *Teaching Digital Natives: Partnering for Real Learning.* Thousand Oaks, CA: Corwin, 2010.

Joel H. Spring — *Education Networks: Power, Wealth, Cyberspace, and the Digital Mind.* New York: Routledge, 2012

Michael Thomas, ed. — *Deconstructing Digital Natives: Young People, Technology, and the New Literacies.* New York: Routledge, 2011.

David Trend — *The End of Reading: From Gutenberg to Grand Theft Auto.* New York: Peter Lang, 2010.

David L. Ulin — *The Lost Art of Reading: Why Books Matter in a Distracted Time.* Seattle: Sasquatch, 2010.

Andrew A. Zucker — *Transforming Schools with Technology: How Smart Use of Digital Tools Helps Achieve Six Key Education Goals.* Cambridge, MA: Harvard Education Press, 2008.

Periodicals and Internet Sources

Spencer E. Ante   "Trying to Avert a Digital Horror Story," *Business Week*, January 11, 2010.

Jonathan Band   "A Guide for the Perplexed: Libraries and the Google Library Project Settlement," Association of Research Libraries, November 23, 2008. www.arl.org.

Nic Boshart   "Brave New Book World," *Alternatives Journal*, May/June 2011.

Julie Bosman   "The Bookstore's Last Stand," *New York Times*, January 28, 2012.

James H. Burnett   "E-books Bringing New Power to the Printed Word," *Miami Herald*, November 15, 2008.

Erin Carreiro   "Electronic Books: How Digital Devices and Supplementary New Technologies Are Changing the Face of the Publishing Industry," *Publishing Research Quarterly*, December 2010.

Jeffrey R. Di Leo   "Green Books," *American Book Review*, March/April 2009.

Ann Dixon   "From Touchstones to Touch Screens: The Evolution of a Book Lover," *Horn Book Magazine*, March/April 2012.

William C. Dougherty	"Managing Technology: E-readers, Passing Fad or Trend of the Future?" *Journal of Academic Librarianship*, May 2010.
Ross Duncan	"Ebooks and Beyond: The Challenge for Public Libraries," *APLIS*, June 2010.
Stephanie Findlay	"From E-books to No Books," *Maclean's*, October 11, 2010.
William Germano	"What Are Books Good For?" *Chronicle of Higher Education*, October 1, 2010.
Hardy Green	"Pulpless Fiction," *Business Week*, June 23, 2008.
Harvard Crimson	"Expanding Education: Harvard's Initiatives Toward Online Book Lending and Education Are Steps in the Right Direction," May 24, 2012.
Miguel Helft	"Microsoft to Stop Scanning Books," *New York Times*, May 24, 2008.
Jamie E. Helgren	"Booking to the Future," *American Libraries*, January/February 2011.
Andrea James	"Books a Weighty Issue for Law Schools," *Seattle Post-Intelligencer*, September 11, 2008.
Kevin Kelly	"From Print to Pixel," *Smithsonian*, July/August 2010.
Wallace Koehler	"Good and Evil in the Garden of Digitization," *Searcher*, June 2008.

Nicole Krauss — "Writer's Block," *New Republic*, March 24, 2011.

Erik Larson — "Authors to Consider Google Deal," *Boston Globe*, April 29, 2009.

Chuck Leddy — "The Changing Future of Books," *Writer*, April 2010.

Claire Lekwa — "Books Not So 'E-easily' Accepted," *Daily Iowan*, May 15, 2008.

Steven Levy — "The Future of Reading," *Newsweek*, November 26, 2007.

Molly Marsh — "Are Books Obsolete?" *Sojourners*, May 2009.

Patrick McCormick — "What Happens at the End of the Book?" *U.S. Catholic*, August 2009.

Jim Milliot — "Catching the Digital Wave," *Publishers Weekly*, March 5, 2012.

Rob Nugent — "The Decline of Reading in an Age of Ignorance," *Quadrant*, January 2011.

Peter Osnos — "Rise of the Reader: How Books Got Wings," *Columbia Journalism Review*, March/April 2009.

John Podhoretz — "The Tolstoy App," *Commentary*, February 2010.

David Pogue — "The Trouble with E-readers," *Scientific American*, November 2010.

Ralph Raab   "Books and Literacy in the Digital Age," *American Libraries*, August 2010.

Pamela Samuelson   "A Universal Digital Library Is Within Reach," *Los Angeles Times*, May 1, 2012.

Jonathan Segura   "No More E-Books vs. Print Books Arguments, OK?" *Monkey See*, January 31, 2012. www.npr.org/blogs /monkeysee.

Ramin Setoodeh and Jennie Yabroff   "The Future of the Book," *Newsweek*, February 14, 2011.

Margaret Simons   "Reading in an Age of Change," *Overland*, Fall 2010.

William Skidelsky   "Death of the Book?" *New Statesman*, September 29, 2008.

Charlie Sorrel   "Is the iPad Driving E-Book Piracy, and Does It Matter?" *Wired*, May 17, 2010.

Tom Spring   "E-Book Piracy: Is Your Download Legitimate?" *PC World*, March 2010.

Brian T. Sullivan   "Academic Library Autopsy Report, 2050," *Chronicle of Higher Education*, January 2, 2011.

Dan Tonkery   "The iPad and Its Possible Impact on Publishers and Libraries," *Searcher*, October 2010.

Priti Trivedi   "Writing the Wrong: What the
                     E-book Industry Can Learn from
                     Digital Music's Mistakes with DRM,"
                     Journal of Law & Policy, 2010.

Emily Williams   "Copyright, E-books and the
                     Unpredictable Future," *Publishing
                     Research Quarterly*, March 2011.

Index

A

Adobe CS4 for Photographers, 72

Advances, for professional writers, 29–30

Alfred P. Sloan Foundation, 60

All-information-is-online, myth, 17

Amazon
backlist titles and, 24
complaints against, 13
creative destruction by, 55–56
digitized book monopoly, 24–25
e-book sales, 28
Kindle Direct Publishing service, 38
Kindle Fire, 88
Kindle reader, 76, 78, 81, 87, 91
Kindle Singles, 88
as the long tail, 31
movie rentals, 64
pricing strategy of, 22–24

American Academy of Publishers, 76

Anderson, Chris, 30, 31, 34

Anti-copyright beliefs, 73

Apple
environmental concerns, 83–84
iPod Touches, 91
iTunes, 23, 31, 64, 69, 74
as publisher, 32, 74
US Justice Department suit against, 22–23, 25, 25n1
See also iPad

Application program interface (API), 61, 62, 64–65

Arcadia Fund, 60

Auel, Jean, 77

Australia, 82

Authors
blogs/blogging by, 34
concerns over digitized books, 13–14
publishing industry and, 29–30
See also Professional writers

Authors Guild, 68

B

Backlist titles, 12, 24

Bantam Dell, 12

Barnes and Noble, 28, 33

Bauman, Zygmunt, 34–35

Bennett, Alan, 73

Bertelsmann media, 28, 35

Bibles, printing of, 10

Blogs/blogging
by authors, 34
content of, 32
criticism of, 19, 44
messages exchanged by, 17
pirating concerns, 73

Bloom, Harold, 93

Book copy, 10

Book Industry Environmental Council (BIEC), 80–81

Book-is-dead myth, 16

Book of the Month Club, 11

Book piracy. See Piracy concerns

Book Rights Registry, 52